DATE DUE

DEMCO, INC. 38-2931

FENG SHUI
for today's living

FENG SHUI
for today's living

MARY LAMBERT

CICO BOOKS
LONDON NEW YORK

First published in 2008 by CICO Books

an imprint of Ryland Peters & Small

519 Broadway, 5th Floor, New York NY 10012

www.cicobooks.com

10 9 8 7 6 5 4 3 2

A CIP catalog record for this book is available from the Library of Congress

ISBN-13: 978 1 906094 30 0

ISBN-10: 1 906094 30 6

Printed in China

Editor: Alison Wormleighton

Designer: Liz Sephton

Illustrators: Trina Dalziel, Cathy Brear, Stephen Dew

CONTENTS

Introduction

Feng shui, which translates as "wind" and "water," is the ancient art of furniture placement and energy flow in the home. Practiced successfully in China for thousands of years, it is now becoming more widely used in the West as people who have implemented feng shui principles have discovered the benefits of a lighter, more positive atmosphere in their homes.

By increasing energy flow, those who have introduced feng shui to their homes have improved their general well-being and family relationships. In addition, they have enhanced other areas of their lives such as their career, love life, and financial prospects. The underlying principle in feng shui is that if you improve your home, it is also reflected both in your body and in your spirit.

How does feng shui work?

Feng shui (pronounced "fung shway" in English) is based on the belief that energy meridians, known as chi (pronounced "chee" in English), flow through the home. These invisible electromagnetic currents need to move freely for there to be a happy and balanced atmosphere. If the currents meet blockages such as clutter or too much furniture,

BELOW A sociable arrangement of the furniture in your living space will allow chi to flow through to all areas in a positive manner.

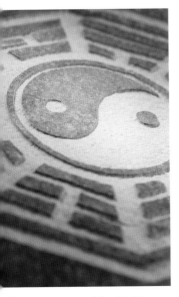

the chi flow will be impeded, making it stilted or sluggish. This can have a detrimental effect on everyone living in the home. If clutter is not cleared out, you will feel lethargic and stuck in a rut.

Once any clutter has been removed, "space clearing" will help to purify the atmosphere. Most people after they have performed a space-clearing ceremony liken it to having spring-cleaned the home—the air feels lighter and more uplifting.

Yin and yang

A fundamental part of feng shui is the balancing of the opposing forces yin and yang. Yin is female, dark, and passive; while yang is seen as everything male, bright, and positive. The t'ai chi symbol (pictured left and on page 17) shows the unity of yin and yang—one cannot exist without the other.

In the home, yin and yang must be balanced for perfect harmony. In your living area, for example, you need to balance hard yang items such as hardwood tables, mirrors, and glass vases with soft yin pillows, curtains, throws, and rugs. If you have too many yin or yang accessories, there will be an energy imbalance.

The five elements and the Pa Kua

The Chinese believe that we are surrounded by five elements: Fire, Wood, Water, Earth, and Metal. The elements are linked to core chi energies, color, and compass directions, and are a refinement of yin and yang. The relationships between these elements, their directions, and the Pa Kua are central to feng shui practice. By knowing how the elements interact in different cycles, the feng shui practitioner can tell you the color needed for each room and suggest how to improve the atmosphere and bring in good luck.

The feng shui practitioner's main diagnostic tool is an eight-sided figure called a Pa Kua, which is used for mapping out the rooms in your home.

FIRE

EARTH

WATER

METAL

WOOD

ABOVE AND RIGHT The five elements: Fire, Metal, Wood, Water, and Earth are an integral part of feng shui practice and can be brought into the home in many different forms. By using different element cycles, energy can be manipulated to create the best atmosphere in the home.

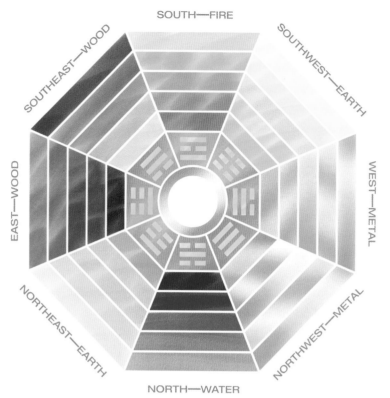

SOUTH—FIRE

SOUTHEAST—WOOD

SOUTHWEST—EARTH

EAST—WOOD

WEST—METAL

NORTHEAST—EARTH

NORTHWEST—METAL

NORTH—WATER

The Pa Kua relates each room to the five elements. Each of the Pa Kua's eight potent trigrams is associated with a different aspect of life. These eight life aspirational spaces, such as Career, or Family and Health, are the areas that can be boosted to improve your life circumstances. By placing the Pa Kua on a plan of each room, you can identify where these eight spaces are in that room.

Practicing feng shui yourself

The first part of this book, *Boost Your Chi Using Feng Shui,* discusses the basic aspects of feng shui and explains how chi, the five elements, and the opposing forces of yin and yang are central to the practice.

Following this look at the fundamental principles of feng shui, you are shown how to employ the Pa Kua yourself to boost the chi in your home and thereby improve your life. The book explains how to use a basic orienteering

ABOVE The Pa Kua is the main feng shui diagnostic tool. It allows you to find out where your life aspirational spaces are in each room. By energizing these spaces, good fortune and success can come your way.

RIGHT Planning your living space following feng shui principles can be fun. Improving the energy flow will lighten the atmosphere and make you feel happier in the space.

compass to take the directions of the rooms in your home, so that with the Pa Kua you can draw up a plan of each room identifying your life aspirational spaces. This will enable you to enhance the relevant ones for your current life's circumstances. So, for example, if money always seems to flow straight out of your bank account, you could try boosting your Wealth and Prosperity space with crystals and special symbols to increase your finances.

Finally, this section of the book gives you practical advice on decluttering your home and removing stagnancy to optimize chi flow, and then cleansing all the rooms using different space-clearing procedures.

Planning your home's interiors

Once you have understood the principles of feng shui and drawn up all the plans of your home, you can start to have fun planning your interiors. This is where the book's second section, *Interior Decorate with Feng Shui*, comes in. Each room in the home, plus the garden, is discussed, and advice on how to plan the layout of each room is given. Guidance is also included on how to improve energy flow and correct any negative features such as beams that send out cutting chi or "poison arrows" coming off sharp corners on furniture.

For each room there are up to four Accessories Files, which are designed to help you furnish that room with a feng shui slant. For example, in the living room chapter you will find tips on sourcing the right color and the most comfortable style of sofa for your room. In the bathroom chapter you will discover how the different shapes and materials of sinks affect the movement of energy there, depending upon whether the room has an Earth, Wood, Fire, Water, or Metal entrance.

Using feng shui techniques can literally change

your life for the better, but don't attempt too much at once. Start with just one room and feel the benefit of what you have put into practice before you move on to other rooms. When you have finished your whole home, you will be amazed at how much better the atmosphere feels and how many different doors open to new opportunities in all aspects of your life.

ABOVE Finding out the best places to put your furniture and the colors that will support your living room will improve this relaxation space.

RIGHT Choosing a comfortable sofa in colors that will enhance or calm your living room will make you feel happy and at peace.

BOOST YOUR CHI USING FENG SHUI

FENG SHUI IS AN ANCIENT CHINESE DISCIPLINE that can have a profound effect on your home and environment and, in so doing, can also have a strong effect on you, because your mind, body, and emotions reflect your home—they mirror each other. Once you understand how feng shui works and start to put the principles into action, you will notice a lighter atmosphere in your home and feel a positive lift in your body. Before you start using the Pa Kua to find and boost your life aspirational spaces, clear out any clutter from your home and cleanse the atmosphere. This will insure that you are working with a neutral blueprint, making it as easy as possible to positively change your life and increase your well-being.

✦ How feng shui works
✦ The five elements
✦ Using the life aspirational spaces
✦ The best feng shui cures and enhancements
✦ The Pa Kua
✦ How to draw plans of your home
✦ Clearing out your junk

How Feng Shui Works

Feng shui is part of Traditional Chinese Medicine along with acupuncture and Chinese herbal medicine. It uses the five elements—Earth, Metal, Fire, Water, and Wood—as part of its diagnostic system. The Western world often finds it hard to accept a philosophy and practice based on an ancient system that was originally developed by Chinese farmers to work and live in harmony with the seasons and land surrounding them. But feng shui has worked for thousands of years, and if you use the practice properly, it can truly transform your life.

In the past the ideal location for a home was a sheltered place with supportive hills or mountains behind and flowing rivers in front. A good mix of sun and shade was essential, along with vegetation that thrived. The farmers found that if they lived in harmony with nature their lives worked well, but if they went against their environment, natural disasters befell them. Homes that faced south were considered to be the best as they benefited from the warmth of the sun, while buildings that faced north suffered from harsh winds and bad weather. As feng shui practices became well known, all the Chinese palaces were built facing south.

In China ancestors have always been revered, so feng shui principles started to be used for burial purposes. This was when the Pa Kua (see page 56), the main feng shui diagnostic tool, was introduced. The Chinese believe that the arrangement of the Pa Kua's eight trigrams, or sacred emblems, which also link to the compass directions, are what gives the Pa Kua its power and potency. The placement of the trigrams affects the meaning of the compass directions.

The trigrams originate from the *I Ching*, or Book of Changes, an ancient Chinese book of

cultural practice and traditions. When people were buried, a particular arrangement of the Pa Kua's trigrams, called the Early Heaven, or yin, arrangement was used; it was believed to make

BELOW The Luo Pan is an ancient Chinese compass used in the Compass School of feng shui.

this Pa Kua arrangement a potent protective symbol. Signifying the ideal universe, it was preferred for yin burial places for loved ancestors. The yin arrangement is still used today in Pa Kua mirrors to counteract bad environmental factors, such as a road being directly opposite the front door.

For modern homes, however, the Later Heaven, or yang, arrangement of the Pa Kua's trigrams is used to map out the spaces, as very positive energy is needed to make a home vibrant. In today's world many of the ancient practices are hard to carry out exactly. This is especially the case in built-up cities, where roads and the shapes of buildings and other man-made structures add another dimension to the feng shui analysis of what is considered to be a good location.

ABOVE The Pa Kua is a potent feng shui tool. Each of the eight segments relates to a life aspirational space, such as Marriage and Romantic Happiness, which can be energized to boost your relationship.

ABOVE The Early Heaven arrangement of the Pa Kua (blue) and the Later Heaven arrangement (red).

What does feng shui mean?

The two words feng shui literally mean "wind" and "water." All life on this planet is affected by these elements, and they in turn are influenced by chi, a life force or energy that is believed to flow through everything and is contained in all living things. Where chi gathers in abundance, plants, animals, and people thrive. Chi is very concentrated in water, particularly where it flows in a slow but positive manner. Think how cities such as Hong Kong built on harbors have flourished and thrived in trade and commerce. But in arid areas or where water is polluted, chi can stagnate.

So for life to be good, there needs to be a positive flow of chi all around. If chi is flowing well in your home, it will improve your moods, helping you to achieve your aims and current goals. However, if chi is stagnating, it can have a profound effect on you, making you feel depressed, lethargic, and unable to go forward in life.

LEFT Hong Kong has thrived commercially because it is situated on a harbor, which means that the water flow around it is strong and full of chi.

What exactly is chi?

Chi is energy: the invisible, subtle electromagnetic energy that circulates everywhere and is in everything. Positive energy is known as sheng chi and its negative form is called sha chi. The Chinese refer to chi as the cosmic dragon's breath. The dragon symbolizes good luck, and because certain beneficial landscape formations resemble the dragon's shape, they have always been associated with good energy flow and good fortune.

In the home, chi enters through the front door in spiral fashion, moving through the home and exiting through the windows. The movement of the energy needs to be positive to have a beneficial effect on all the people living there. Unfortunately, the surrounding environment and the home's layout can disrupt this flow, which can then adversely affect the occupants' health. Straight roads or paths facing the front door, as well as single trees, lampposts, and sharp corners, can create negative energy, or sha chi.

Inside the home, piles of clutter will also disrupt the energy flow, making it sluggish and lethargic. If the clutter has been there a long time, the energy will be very musty and stagnant. Beams, pillars, and sharp or deep corners on walls or furniture can cause the chi to spin wildly,

creating "poison arrows," or sha chi. This can make people in the home feel depressed unless cures are put in place. If doors are facing each other in halls or foyers, chi will speed up and you will lose its beneficial effects. By harmonizing the chi flow you can make your home a much brighter and more pleasant place to live.

What feng shui can do for you

The energy flowing through the home relates to its atmosphere. How many times have you walked into a dark, dismal house and found it cold, oppressive, and uninviting, while in a bright, sunny home you feel welcome and your spirit soars? When a feng shui consultant visits, they will put the feng shui blueprint on your home and will be able to sense where there are energy blockages because of piles of clutter, overcrowded surfaces, dull corners, or possibly lingering negative energies from previous occupants.

Before you knew about feng shui you may have had discordant colors, badly placed furniture, and negative areas such as sharp corners, pillars, or

ABOVE Keeping a kitchen/diner clutter-free will aid the flow of chi, as the energy can move easily around the room without obstruction, to exit through the window.

BELOW Chi is believed to represent the cosmic dragon's breath. In Chinese culture dragons are believed to bring good fortune.

ABOVE The Chinese are great believers in luck, and by using feng shui you can attract good fortune into your life.

BELOW Rounded seating and side tables aid the flow of chi. Red furniture links to the Fire element and can strengthen a Fire living room or bring some calming energy into a Wood living room.

beams in your home creating an unbalanced atmosphere without your even realizing it. This disturbed atmosphere will have impacted on your family life and how you all interacted, often causing upset, arguments, unhappiness, continuous problems, bickering, and niggling aggravations.

Once you appreciate the principles of feng shui you will begin to understand how it can improve your life. By manipulating the flow of energy, changing the color of each room to link to its element, moving furniture into more auspicious spaces, employing cures to offset negative influences, and using enhancements in positive areas, you can change your home into a lighter, more harmonious place to live and bring opportunities, happiness, and joy into your life.

Chinese luck

Luck has always been viewed as capricious in the West, where it is likened to the chances of winning the lottery. For the Chinese, however, it is seen as something to be encouraged and developed, which can partly be in your control. The ancient Chinese believed there are three types of luck:

+ First there is the luck that you are born with and that obviously relates to the family you are born into; this is called "Heaven luck."
+ The second type of luck is the luck we make for ourselves by working hard in our lives and careers; this is called "Man luck."
+ The third kind of luck, "Earth luck," is the type you acquire by skillfully using the feng shui principles. By boosting the chi of different life aspirational areas of the Pa Kua, such as the Family or Love space, you can encourage good fortune and happiness into these spaces.

Applying feng shui principles

Feng shui is an intricate practice and should not be played with. By working with the formulas, you can increase good fortune and have a smoother path in life, but you must follow the practice carefully. If you learn just a small amount and cannot be bothered to understand all the intricacies, you may apply it incorrectly, and then fortune can turn against you just as quickly as it can turn in your favor. If you do not have time to learn the feng shui techniques properly, you may be better off calling in an experienced consultant to help you understand how to make the most of your home.

Feng shui is not a religion, it is a spiritual practice that has its roots in Taoist beliefs. Once you have learned the principles, you will find that your intuition increases and you become more in tune with yourself, so that you will be able to read your home more easily. You will see from the style you have chosen and the art you are displaying on the walls what is going on in your mind, as one reflects the other. Feng shui is a science, an art, and a specialized practice that can create balance, harmony, and contentment in your life and home.

BALANCING YIN AND YANG

One of the major parts of feng shui and the way the Chinese view earth energies is the balancing of the opposing or complementary forces of yin and yang—one cannot exist without the other.

These two terms work together to compare everything that exists or is alive. Yin is seen as being female, dark, negative, cold, wet, passive/still, weak, and soft, while yang is considered to be male, bright, positive, warm, dry, active, strong, and determined. Yin is the earth, the moon, nighttime, water, the valley, and death, while yang is associated with heaven, the sun, daylight, fire,

mountains, and life. As regards colors, blue, violet, green, and black are at the yin end of the spectrum, while reds, pinks, and oranges are at the yang end.

Yin and yang constantly interact. You can see it in how the soft moon changes into the bright sun and how darkness becomes light, as well as in the seasons and how the warmth and

ABOVE Calm and passive, yin energy is represented by the soft light of the moon that fills the sky at night.

BELOW Always balance yin and yang energy. This fluffy yin rug offsets the harder yang energy of the furniture.

BELOW A mantelpiece is a good place to display a selection of pebbles, ceramic vases, and plants in order to add some yang energy to a more yin living room.

ABOVE A peaceful stone Buddha brings in some yang energy to a room, as well as representing a calm oasis.

brightness of the yang summer give way to the darker, cold yin winter. Neither can be seen as good or bad—they must be viewed in terms of how they relate to each other.

In ancient times the ideal home location was chosen with yin and yang in mind. A warm, sunny, yang, south-facing site protected by the colder, yin shade of a north-facing mountain or hill, with faster, flowing yang water energy in front, was considered the best place to live.

The t'ai chi symbol

The Taoist t'ai chi symbol shows the relationship of yin and yang. The white section represents the positive, bright, yang energy, while the black section shows the passive, darker, yin energy. They are united in a circle, both blending into each other to show their codependency. However,

within each section there is a small circle of the opposing energy, denoting how nothing is ever completely yin or yang.

Using yin and yang in the home

When you are looking at the yin and yang balance in your home, yang energy should dominate in a 3:2 ratio. Growing children require positive yang energy to develop. Where an elderly person is living or a sick person is convalescing, there must be a strong yang presence to keep the body healthy or help it to heal. Yang energy is very vibrant and it can also attract good fortune, whereas bringing in too much yin energy can attract loss, lethargy, or illness. But a good proportion of yin energy is still important, as we need to restore ourselves in our homes and to feel safe and protected there.

Ultimately, creating the right balance of yin and yang brings perfect harmony, but this will vary in each room, depending on how it is used:

✦ **The entry hall** requires a strong presence of yang energy to encourage energy into the home. Mirrors and good lighting can help to increase its presence.

✦ **The living room** is a more flexible place. If you are older, you may want a higher presence of yang energy to keep you vibrant, but most people prefer a stronger level of yin energy for calmness and relaxation. You can balance the "harder" yang furniture such as hardwood tables with "softer" yin pieces such as a comfortable sofa (see also chart opposite). Bringing in more throws, pillows, and hangings will increase the yin presence.

✦ **The bedroom** needs a calm and nurturing atmosphere, as this is where you give your body and spirit a well-deserved rest. Fill the room with tactile yin pillows and bedding, fluffy rugs, and flowing curtains.

✦ **A child's bedroom**, too, should be a yin environment, but because it often doubles as a playroom or study, it may have zoned areas: a yin sleeping space with fun patterned bedding and comfortable carpet or wool rugs, and a yang area for working at a computer, listening to music, playing with toys and electronic games, or entertaining friends. Placing a screen between the two areas will help to keep the energies separated.

✦ **The bathroom** is where you want to relax and wash away the worries of the day, so balance out the hard yang sink, bath, and shower fixtures with yin fluffy towels and bathmats.

LEFT Soft, flowing sofas and throws exude yin energy to contrast with the harder yang energy of the walls and floor.

✦ **The dining room** should be a very yang room with a vibrant atmosphere as it is where the family eats and friends are entertained. To keep the presence of yang energy high here, you could display your wine glasses and china, and use candles in ceramic holders, as these are all yang accessories.

✦ **The kitchen** is considered the heart of the home. It is where family meals are prepared and often eaten, so the yang energy needs to be higher. Sinks, granite, laminate, or hardwood counters and hardwood cabinets will increase yang energies. These can be softened with some yin energy from cushions on chairs, dish towels, or wicker baskets.

ABOVE The soft, yin lines of a leather sofa can offset yang modular storage pieces in your living room.

LEFT Increase the conviviality of lunches and dinners by boosting the yang energy on your dining table with wine glasses and ceramic tableware.

Yin and yang checklist for each room

Room	Yang furniture and accessories	Yin furniture and accessories
ENTRY HALL	Mirrors; lighting; hardwood coatstand; metal plant holders	Carpet or rugs; softwood flooring
LIVING ROOM	Hardwood, glass, or metal furniture; stone or ceramic statues; shutters; marble or stone floors	Upholstered furniture; cotton, suede, or velvet pillows; carpet or rugs; wool, fake fur, or cotton throws; wicker or rattan furniture
DINING ROOM	Round hardwood or glass table; hardwood or metal chairs; mirror; wine glasses and flatware; dinner plates	Rectangular or oval softwood table; softwood dining chairs with upholstered seats; fabric tablecloths; silk or linen runners; fabric or rush placemats
KITCHEN	Hardwood kitchen units and counters; ceramic, glass, or slate tiles; stone floor; granite, marble, or laminate counters; hardwood butcher block; plastic Venetian blinds	Softwood kitchen units and counters; linoleum, vinyl, or rubber flooring; softwood stools or chairs with rattan or rush seats; curtains or shades; wicker baskets; dish towels
BEDROOM	Hardwood bed; bedside cabinets or tables; plastic, metal, or hardwood Venetian blinds; glass-framed pictures; hardwood floor	Bedlinen, comforter, pillows, bedspreads; wicker or rattan furniture; curtains or shades; carpets or rugs
CHILD'S BEDROOM	Hardwood floor and cupboards; wooden bed; plastic and wooden toys; computer equipment; plastic storage boxes; electronic games, CDs, and DVDs; stereo	Carpet; soft wool, cotton, or rag rugs; patterned curtains; furry toy animals; fabric or paper screen; character bedlinen and bedcover; fabric pajama case; floor pillows
BATHROOM	Ceramic bathroom fixtures; ceramic, stone, or glass floor tiles; mirror; light fixtures; ceramic or stone wall tiles; plastic or metal Venetian blinds; plants	Fluffy towels and bathrobes; linoleum, vinyl, or rubber flooring; shades; bathmats and rugs; wicker or softwood cabinets; natural sponges and loofahs

The Five Elements

The Chinese believe that by combining all the five elements—Fire, Metal, Water, Earth, and Wood—you can create all the different permutations that are found in nature. An integral part of feng shui practice, the interaction of these elements is used in the layout of the home or office to bring about good luck for the occupants.

Each of the five elements represents one of the main chi energies, which are refinements of yin and yang and link to the Pa Kua (see page 56), feng shui's main diagnostic tool. Each element matches up to a compass direction, a color, a potent trigram, and a life aspiration. For example, Fire relates to the south, red, *li* and Recognition and Fame, while Water links to the north, blue/black, *k'an* and Career. How the five elements relate to the Pa Kua is at the heart of feng shui practice.

The five-element cycles

The elements are controlled by two interactive cycles: the Productive and Destructive.

+ In the Productive (feeding) cycle each element produces the next element (see diagram) in complete harmony, so Fire produces Earth, which produces Metal, which produces Water, which produces Wood, which produces Fire, and so on.

+ The Destructive (controlling) cycle shows the ongoing process of decay that is everywhere in nature. In this cycle Water destroys (or puts out) Fire, which destroys (or melts) Metal, which destroys (or chops down) Wood, which destroys (or breaks up) Earth, which destroys (or absorbs) Water.

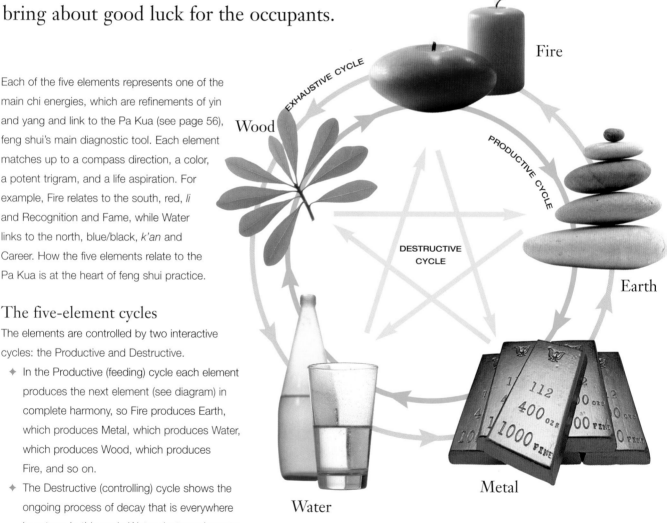

Fire

Wood

EXHAUSTIVE CYCLE

PRODUCTIVE CYCLE

DESTRUCTIVE CYCLE

Earth

Metal

Water

ABOVE The five-element cycle is used by feng shui consultants to adjust energy flow in each room, creating harmony and balance in the home.

Using the elements in your home

Either paint the room "neutral" (matching the element associated with the room's orientation—see pages 58–59) or use the colors related to the calming element in living rooms, bathrooms, and bedrooms for more relaxation, and the colors related to the energizing element in entry halls, dining rooms, studies, and kitchens for more vibrancy. Here are the neutral, calming, and energizing colors for each element:

ABOVE Red is the vibrant color that will enhance a Fire room. Alternatively, it can be used to energize an Earth dining room, entry hall, kitchen, or study.

There are two other cycles that also play a major part in feng shui analysis:

- ✦ The Exhaustive (calming) cycle is the reverse of the Productive cycle.
- ✦ The Clashing (draining) cycle is the opposite of the Destructive cycle.

The interpretation of all these cycles is important for harmony and balance in the home. The aim is to use them to select the colors to decorate a room once you have worked out the orientation of the room (see page 58), since each orientation is associated with an element. When decorating using feng shui principles, the colours linked to a particular element are "neutral"; the colors linked to the element that feeds it (in the Productive cycle) are "energizing"; those linked to the element that calms it (in the Exhaustive cycle) are "calming," and so on. To make an ideal living space, try to use the neutral, energizing, or calming colors in a room and keep to a minimum the ones that control (Destructive cycle) or drain (Clashing cycle).

Element	Decorate with color
FIRE	To *keep neutral*, use shades of red from crimson through oranges to pinks and peaches.
	To *calm*, use shades of yellow from bright yellow through lemons and saffrons to pale beige. To *energize*, use shades of green from a moss green through lime and olive greens to a soft mint.
EARTH	To *keep neutral*, use shades of yellow (see above).
	To *calm*, use shades of white from a violet or blue white to a soft white; you can also use gold and silver. To *energize*, use shades of red (see above).
METAL	To *keep neutral*, use shades of white (see above).
	To *calm*, use shades of blue from a strong midnight blue through steel blue and turquoise to a soft lavender; you can also use shades of black. To *energize*, use shades of yellow (see above).
WATER	To *keep neutral*, use shades of blue and black (see above).
	To *calm*, use shades of green (see above). To *energize*, use shades of white, silver or gold (see above).
WOOD	To *keep neutral*, use shades of green (see above).
	To *calm*, use shades of red (see above). To *energize*, use shades of blue and black (see above).

FIRE

The Fire element links to red, which is a passionate, romantic, and vibrant color that will always make a big impression in a room. Fire is also symbolized by lights and candles, so by placing these in a Fire room you can enhance the existing energies. Fire is associated with the south, the warmth of summer, and the energies of your Recognition and Fame aspirational space (see page 40).

Red is a stimulating color that is believed to bring good fortune and happiness. It can strongly affect our moods, making shy people more courageous, for example, but it can also increase blood pressure and cause anger and aggression if too strong a shade is used.

Red can add vibrancy to a south-facing bedroom but be careful not to use too strong a tone, unless you are young and vital, as you may find it too overwhelming or it may cause your passion to wane. In an entry hall you may want to choose a soft pink or peach shade so that the main entrance to the home stays bright and inviting. To add some more peace into a Fire living room, paint it a tone of yellow and add some fabrics in a matching shade. If you have a Fire study, fill it with energy for creative working by decorating it in a pleasant shade of green and bringing in some wooden furniture.

RIGHT This interesting combination of a wooden table and red chairs brings different energies into a Fire dining room. The wood energizes the room for positive eating, while the red is neutral in a Fire room and so is harmonizing.

10 ways to bring more Fire into a south room

✦ Buy soft furnishings with triangular or star patterns as these signify the Fire element.

✦ Have several star-shaped candle holders.

✦ Bring in a selection of red *objets*.

✦ Scatter pink or red candles around the room.

✦ Place lamps in all the corners of the room.

✦ Have an open fire or fuel-effect fire to enhance the Fire energies.

✦ Comfortable red sofas and chairs strengthen the energy.

✦ Red throws and pillows will emphasize Fire energy.

✦ Silk or wool wall hangings with a red pattern support Fire energy.

✦ Pink, orange, or red flowering plants will lift the room.

BELOW LEFT Red kitchen utensils will give you more Fire energy for cooking in a south kitchen.

ABOVE A rounded red sofa supports the energy in a Fire living room or can calm a Wood living space.

ABOVE Fire is also represented by candles, which can light up a living or dining room.

RIGHT Tactile red and pink pillows will bring Fire energy into a south living room.

EARTH

The Earth element is associated with yellow or beige, which is a cheerful and joyous color, reminiscent of the hot summer sun, lifting your spirits and stimulating your intellect.

Pebbles and china placed in an Earth room will also strengthen this energy. Earth is linked to two directions: the southwest (strong Earth) and the northeast (small Earth). It is also linked to the long, hot days of late summer and the energies of your Marriage and Romantic Happiness (southwest) space and Education and Knowledge (northeast) space (see pages 34 and 42).

Yellow is an inspiring color and can help to bring harmony and balance into your life. It can make you feel more able to make decisions and more focused on your goals and ambitions, but avoid shades with a greenish tinge as they can increase irritability and may slightly raise blood pressure.

Painting a northeast or southwest bathroom a sunny yellow brings in its powerful vibrations, which will help to wake up a sleepy brain in the

ABOVE A modern yellow-patterned rug will strengthen the Earth energies in a living room in the southwest or northeast.

LEFT Pebbles are very obvious Earth symbols that can also bring in grounding energy.

morning. Using a lemon yellow in a bright and sunny southwest dining room will add a slightly fresher, cooler appeal for long, leisurely lunches during the summer months. In an Earth room where you primarily want to relax or perhaps meditate, bring in a shade of calming white to lower the vibrations. If you want to liven up an Earth kitchen, paint it a warm shade of red and add some extra lighting to give it more "buzz."

ABOVE Bring the bright yellow color of the Earth element into a room by displaying some beautiful yellow flowers.

LEFT Stone ornaments, such as this angel statue, are a good way of bringing energy into an Earth room.

ABOVE Ceramic tea sets are also Earth energy that can support southwest and northeast kitchens.

10 ways to bring more Earth into a northeast or southwest room

✦ Place grounding pebbles around the room.

✦ A selection of different crystals supports the Earth energy.

✦ Buy curtain or upholstery fabrics in square, striped, or rectangular designs as these also relate to the Earth element.

✦ Display patterned square or rectangular plates on the wall.

✦ Include comfortable beige sofas.

✦ Feature a china cabinet in either of these rooms.

✦ Bring in yellow rugs or beige carpeting.

✦ Put yellow rectangular photo frames around the room.

✦ Yellow flowers strengthen Earth energies.

✦ Yellow tablecloths and napkins enhance Earth energies.

ABOVE Citrine is a wonderful golden stone of abundance that can adorn an Earth room.

RIGHT Beige links to the Earth element, so you can use beige sofas, pillows, and throws in an Earth living room.

METAL

The Metal element connects to white. It is a pure, protective color that helps us develop and makes rooms seem more open and spacious. Gold, silver, and metallic objects also link to Metal to bring in more of these solid, grounding energies.

Metal is associated with two directions: the west (small Metal) and the northwest (strong Metal). It is also associated with the late autumn at the end of the rich growing season and the energies of your Children and Projects (west) space and Mentors and Networking (northwest) space (see pages 44 and 46).

Metal is a consistent and reliable element that can bring a cleansing of the mind, body, and spirit. In feng shui it represents money in the bank and what we can achieve with our own efforts. White promotes physical energy, but avoid displaying too much pure white in your home because it can encourage feelings of isolation and can restrict how you make decisions.

Using a soft white with gold or silver accents in a small west or northwest living room will make it seem bigger and full of light. White is also a spiritual color, so using a violet white in a west bathroom will make it a very relaxing place to retreat to after an exhausting day. Painting a Metal bedroom a soft blue will have a calming effect and help with sleeping problems. For more stimulating energy in a Metal office, paint it a rich golden yellow, which will increase concentration and creative skills.

LEFT A metal statue such as this Buddha can bring in a feeling of calm, enhancing the Metal energies in a living room in the northwest or west.

10 ways to bring more Metal into a west or northwest room

- ✦ Include tall iron candlesticks in the room.
- ✦ Put up pictures with metal picture frames.
- ✦ Buy soft furnishings that have oval or circular patterns, as they are also associated with the Metal element.
- ✦ Choose white cotton or leather upholstery for sofas.
- ✦ Silver or gold bowls support Metal energy.
- ✦ Put vases of white flowers around the room.
- ✦ White fluffy rugs enhance Metal energy.
- ✦ Place metal plant containers in the corners of the room.
- ✦ Put round white pillows in a metallic-patterned fabric on the sofas or chairs.
- ✦ Position a metal Buddha in the northwest corner of the room—the Mentors and Networking space.

ABOVE When your kitchen has a Metal orientation, use copper or stainless steel saucepans to display the Metal element.

BELOW A bronze-colored throw can be used in a bedroom or living room to display the Metal element.

BELOW A white sofa and white accessories create a clean, peaceful effect to strengthen the energies in a Metal living room.

ABOVE If you want to bring more Metal energy into a room, metal candlesticks or other accessories will increase its presence.

WATER

The Water element is denoted by blue or black. Blue brings to mind a beautiful sky in summer or the calmness of a still, turquoise sea. Its coolness helps us to relax and take life at a more leisurely pace.

Inevitably, the Water element also connects to flowing water, so if you place a water feature in a Water room you are balancing the existing energies there. Water is associated with the north, the cold and chill of winter, and the energies of your Career aspirational space (see page 33).

Blue is a soothing color. Emotionally it can help to release tension and help you unwind, though the darker shades can sometimes increase depressive tendencies. Water is seen as a positive activator that can help us accumulate wealth, increasing our prosperity, as it is always moving positive chi around the home.

A soft blue shade can increase the tranquil atmosphere of a north bedroom, as this is where we recover from the trials of the day. A powder

ABOVE A cool blue sofa, harmonizing pillows, and some blue or black accessories display the Water energy needed in a living room in the north.

LEFT Cut flowers or flowering plants with a blue hue link to Water and can be displayed in a north living room.

blue shade in a Water living room creates a cool and airy space for relaxed conversation and entertaining. To lend more tranquility to a north shower room, paint it a leaf or sage green.

To lift the ambience in a Water entry hall, add some metal accessories, then paint it white with a hint of blue and see how much lighter and more spacious the entry hall looks.

10 ways to bring more Water energy into a north room

✦ Site an aquarium or running water feature in the room, ideally in the southeast to boost your Wealth space.

✦ Buy soft furnishings and fabrics with wavy or cloudlike patterns as these symbolize the Water element.

✦ Scatter blue ornaments on windowsills and shelving.

✦ Display some black carved statues.

✦ Feature bowls of blue flowers.

✦ Blue flowing curtains in light muslin or tactile velvet augment Water energy.

✦ A wavy-shaped black coffee table suggests the presence of Water.

✦ Put different fruits in a series of black bowls.

✦ A cabinet of wine glasses increases Water energy.

✦ Include comfortable blue chairs.

LEFT If you have a Water kitchen, have pitchers of water around to increase the element energies existing here.

ABOVE An aquarium or goldfish bowl is a wonderful enhancement in a Water living room. The movement of the fish activates the flow of chi in the room, particularly if you choose lively ones.

ABOVE AND RIGHT Black or blue dinnerware looks stylish and will bring in beneficial Water chi for family meals and dinner parties.

WOOD

The Wood element relates to the color green, which is a restful and balancing hue that is neither warm nor cold. Wooden floors, accessories, and furniture can be used in a room to attract more of this calming, grounded energy, as can houseplants, which also make up the Wood element.

Wood links to two directions: the east (strong Wood) and the southeast (small Wood). It is also associated with the promise of the new growing season in spring and the energies of your Family and Health (east) space and Wealth and Prosperity (southeast) space (see pages 36 and 38).

Green is a compassionate, calm, and very passive color. It is a great healer of the emotions, particularly soothing heartache, but be careful with muddy greens as they can encourage lethargy and boredom.

Decorating an east or southeast breakfast room in green can promote harmony, as its relaxing shades will help prevent bickering or family upsets. In a sunroom, a soft fern green will emphasize the feeling of nature, bringing the beauty of the garden indoors. In a bedroom, use a soft pink or peach for a calm, relaxed atmosphere. To help with creative thinking in a Wood study, decorate the room in a mid-blue, such as turquoise or sky blue, and add a water feature to stimulate the vibrations here.

RIGHT A solid hardwood table makes a statement in a Wood dining room in the southeast and east, and brings in positive yang energies.

BELOW Bring more Wood energies into a room by displaying unique pieces of wooden furniture, such as this unusual seat.

RIGHT Carved wooden units from the orient look stunning in a Wood living room and can also serve as a useful focal point.

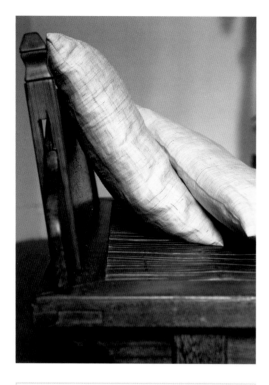

10 ways to bring more Wood into an east or southeast room

✦ Place a rectangular wooden dining table or coffee table in a living space.

✦ Wooden carvings or statues emphasize the Wood element.

✦ Display some wooden photo frames.

✦ Put fruit in wooden bowls around the room.

✦ Round-leaved houseplants will support the Wood element (but not in the bedroom).

✦ A wooden TV stand or CD unit will bring in more Wood energies.

✦ Choose fabrics with a vertical stripe as these also represent the Wood element.

✦ Have some soft pillows in different shades of green.

✦ A display of carved wooden animals accentuates the Wood element.

✦ Use green patterned rugs in the room.

BELOW Green china is associated with Wood and will increase Wood energies in the kitchen or dining room.

RIGHT Houseplants are also the Wood element and will lift the energy and take pollutants out of the atmosphere.

Using the Life Aspirational Spaces

Arranged in a ring around the Pa Kua are eight trigrams, which originate from the ancient Chinese divination book the *I Ching*. These trigrams give a special energetic power to the life aspirational spaces, found on another ring of the Pa Kua.

To help your life to go more smoothly you can activate each area with its associated element. For example, the trigram for the northwest is *chien*, which relates to the Metal element and to the Mentors and Networking space. The trigram for the southeast is *sun* and it links to the Wood element and to the Wealth and Prosperity area. By placing enhancements, symbols, or energizers in all these spaces you can help to bring more wealth into your life, encourage fertility, make your career more successful, or attract that desired romantic partner.

ABOVE Chinese or Indian images of gods can be displayed in your Mentors and Networking space in the northwest.

RIGHT Artifacts such as this wooden elephant can be placed in the southeast to enhance your Wealth and Prosperity area.

CAREER

PA KUA SECTOR:

POSITION:
North

ELEMENT:
Water

SEASON:
Winter

COLOR:
Blue or black

TRIGRAM:
K'an

Your Career space is situated in the north of each room of your home. This is the area of ambition, the space where you can achieve your career dreams and foster your future success. It also symbolizes hard work and believing in your own abilities to get what you truly desire out of your career. If you have a room that faces north, this is the ideal location for a study and you can situate your desk in the northern section of the room. Alternatively, place a desk in the north of a living room or dining room. Avoid having a desk in your bedroom unless this is the only viable space for it as the yin energies there can work against you.

Boosting your Career space

Before you boost your chosen Career area, make sure you are not storing any junk here. Look out for a dilapidated computer or printer, which could hinder your progress. Be aware of any old work files, brochures, or company pictures that connect you with your past life and career and not your present one. Think about what you want out of your present career. If you are feeling very stressed and unappreciated, consider whether you want to

Career activators

To attract the career success you truly want, put the following in the north space of your living room, dining room, or study:

✦ Install a running water feature, or an aquarium with an odd number of goldfish including one black one.

✦ Place your business cards here in a metal box (Metal feeds Water in the element cycle).

✦ Leave your cellphone here overnight to signify a business person who is regularly in touch.

✦ Use a blue desk lamp to increase Water energy.

✦ Place a good professional picture of you in a metal frame, tuck a business card in the back, and put a current resumé under it to fire up your career prospects.

stay in your present position or move on. Write down your current aims for the next year and set some for just a few months ahead so that you have something to work toward.

Putting potent symbols and energizers such as water features or your business cards in this space (see activators, above) will make a statement to the world that you are determined to make a mark in your chosen career.

EDUCATION AND KNOWLEDGE

PA KUA SECTOR:

POSITION:
Northeast

ELEMENT:
Small Earth

SEASON:
Late summer

COLOR:
Yellow or beige

TRIGRAM:
Ken

Your Education and Knowledge space is located in the northeast of each room in your home. This is the place where you acquire more knowledge and where you study different subjects to improve your mind and possibly increase your job prospects. It is also an area that can help you to change career in later life, where job fulfillment can take over from the pursuit of achieving financial gain. This is the area of self-development where your studies can help you find out who you are emotionally, spiritually, and mentally. Bookshelves or a study cabinet can be placed in the northeast of a study, living room, or dining room. They could also be positioned in an entry hall if you have a small apartment. Avoid placing them in a bedroom because of the yin energies existing there.

Boosting your Education and Knowledge space

Before you start putting your energizers and symbols in place, have a look at your chosen northeastern area and see if you have inadvertently left old school textbooks, trophies or certificates of past achievements from school or college, transcripts, diplomas, or school annuals, as these all tie you to the person you once were, rather

RIGHT Fill your space in the northeast with educational books you love and regularly use.

than the person you are now. If they are torn or faded, it is even more important to remove them. Also look for any material relating to courses that you failed or never finished; it may be, say, a yoga brochure, evening class details, or a course prospectus that has been left here. Leaving these items in this space could stop you from wanting to learn something in the near future that is new and more appropriate to your current self. Also remove any self-development books that you have read and learned from but no longer feel are relevant to your life. Remove any discarded craft projects that

Education and Knowledge activators

To create the right environment for your studies, put these articles in the northeastern space of your living room, dining room or study:

✦ Surround the space with any recently acquired diplomas and light them well to give them prominence.

✦ Place language or learning disks here along with a CD- or MP3-player if you are downloading podcasts.

✦ Put a natural quartz crystal here, as it links to the Earth element, increasing your memory skills and learning ability.

✦ Red or pink candles here will stimulate more learning as Fire feeds Earth in the element cycle.

✦ Materials that are needed for an arts and crafts or other self-development class can be left here between sessions to increase creative motivation.

ABOVE Your Education and Knowledge space is all about study and acquiring knowledge.

you have never got around to finishing, to allow for new ones that you do want to complete.

Remember that this space will also affect your children and their studies, so search out any of their old school materials or discarded achievements that have no relevance to their present studies. Even small items such as broken pens and crayons, discarded projects, or unwanted paintings are best removed. If this type of stagnating material is left here, you may find that your children become reluctant to attend school or after-school clubs.

Placing specially chosen symbols and energizers such as crystals or your language or learning disks in this area will speak volumes about your constant desire to acquire new knowledge.

✦ *Put a natural quartz crystal here, as it links to the Earth element.*

RIGHT Keep updating your self-development books as your character develops and your outlook changes.

FAMILY AND HEALTH

PA KUA SECTOR:

POSITION:
East

ELEMENT:
Strong Wood

SEASON:
Spring

COLOR:
Green (also brown)

TRIGRAM:
Chen

Your Family and Health space is situated in the east of each room in your home. This is the place where you forge strong bonds with your romantic partner and your children. It is here that respect and love are nurtured for your parents, grandparents, and other relatives such as aunts, uncles, and cousins. It is also a space that deals with the state of your health, such as how stressed you are and how well you feel on a day-to-day basis. It is about getting enough sleep and rest and managing your health and well-being in a structured way so that you stay balanced and happy. Feature cherished family photos and related pieces on shelves in the east of the living room or bedroom. Health food or supplements and fresh fruit and vegetables are best kept in the eastern space of the kitchen.

Boosting your Family and Health space

Before you energize your chosen Family and Health area with enhancements, check the space to see what you are keeping there. Remove any

RIGHT Your space in the east is also about looking after your body and staying fit by eating well and exercising regularly.

dusty photo albums with faded or torn pictures, as these will diminish the family's energy. Critical letters or cards from upset relatives will also disrupt happy family interaction. Violent novels or books on broken families will feed negativity into the space. If you have a broken or damaged statue here that was perhaps a family holiday memento, it could affect the morale of your family.

The area is also about family health, so beware of leaving here old pill bottles, creams, or discarded cough medicine that the family have used, as these can encourage illness. Your health is precious, so remove any notes on failed exercise plans, details of sports you gave up, diets that did not work, or a bad health assessment from a clinic—only positive symbols should go in this space. Look for other negative symbols, such as bad attendance for sports, old prescriptions for tablets, or a broken thermometer that may be affecting your children's zest for life.

✦ Dumbbells, exercise bands, massage balls, Pilates or yoga DVDs, and vitamin supplements encourage good fitness and overall well-being.

Family and Health activators

To create harmony and balance in your health and family life, place these items in your east space in the living room, bedroom, or kitchen:

✦ Put a healthy round-leaved plant here to strengthen the Wood energies.

✦ A happy family photograph in a rectangular wooden frame will promote good communication in the family.

✦ Fresh fruit and nuts in this area of the kitchen or living room boost good health and a love of healthy foods.

✦ Dumbbells, exercise bands, massage balls, Pilates or yoga DVDs, and vitamin supplements encourage good fitness and overall well-being.

✦ Blue accessories and a flowing water feature or fountain bring in some of the energizing Water element.

Slow, dull vibrations emanating from the Family area will bring about dissatisfaction and upset for no reason, and negatively affect your family's approach to life. They can also deplete your immune system, making you feel sluggish and lethargic.

Positioning vibrant symbols and energizers such as a flourishing round-leaved plant, fresh fruit, and a happy family photograph here will show your commitment to a balanced and healthy family life. You can emphasize the exercise element by placing your yoga DVD, exercise mat, dumbbells, or exercise bands here.

ABOVE Going to the gym regularly is one of the ways you and your family can stay fit and healthy.

WEALTH AND PROSPERITY

POSITION:
Southeast

ELEMENT:
Small Wood

SEASON:
Spring

COLOR:
Green

TRIGRAM:
Sun

Your Wealth and Prosperity space is positioned in the southeast of each room in your home. This is probably your most important life aspiration space as it deals with the finances and overall wealth of everybody living in the home. It is about the financial success that you can achieve in business, financial windfalls that come your way, how you nurture shares or investments for future gain, and the security and stability that you can attain for your family.

But this space is not only about money, as not all of us are destined to be wealthy. It is also about abundance: what you cherish and love in your life. It may be an adored cat or dog, special friends, favorite objects, and collections, or the new opportunities that are waiting to come into your life.

You can create a special wealth shelf or table in most rooms of your home. The one exception

to this is the bathroom, which is constantly draining positive energy, but the living room is an ideal room for it.

Boosting your Wealth and Prosperity space

Before you raise the energetics in your chosen southeastern space, see what you have stored in there at the moment. You may find old bank statements stashed there from a time when you were constantly overdrawn. Or you may discover evidence of a loan you struggled to pay, shares that didn't fare too well, a stagnating savings account statement or details of an overdraft or loan, which are all suggesting that money doesn't flow easily for you. Leaving bills unpaid will insure that money just flies out of your account. Also watch out for any negative pictures that you may be displaying here. Old slavery pictures or

LEFT AND BELOW LEFT
Your Wealth and Prosperity space links to your overall financial success. It is about the money you earn because of your business acumen and how successful you are with investments.

BELOW You can put a bowl of coins in one of your Wealth and Prosperity spaces to show that you will always have money in your life.

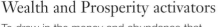

Wealth and Prosperity activators

To draw in the money and abundance that you deserve, display these objects in the southeastern space of your living room or other chosen room:

✦ Grow a healthy jade plant in a clay pot, placing a gold coin in the soil to show how your finances are improving.

✦ Put a trio of money-activating crystals here. The vibrations of rose quartz, citrine, and aventurine will combine to help bring in wealth and success for you.

✦ Store savings bonds, current savings account statements,and lottery tickets here to absorb the positive money energies.

✦ Install a running water feature, or an aquarium containing an uneven number of goldfish—nine is an auspicious number (Water feeds Wood in the element cycle). Have one black fish to absorb any negativity.

✦ Bowls of coins or some notes denote wealth. Also include some of your adored possessions and pictures.

photographs of impoverished tribesmen will say to the world that you find earning money hard work. Dying plants or flowers, a discarded billfold, your dead cat's ashes, or possessions you dislike and keep meaning to throw away can indicate stagnation and a poor flow of money and adversely affect the abundance in your life.

Including special symbols and energizers such as a jade plant, crystals, and current savings account statements to activate money growth will show your true commitment to bringing financial success into your life. Remember that money is just an energy, but there need to be positive vibrations in your Wealth space to attract the prosperity you need. Also add into this area those special treasured items or pictures of adored friends or pets, to allow abundance in these spaces to continue.

✦ *Bowls of coins or some notes denote wealth.*

RECOGNITION AND FAME

PA KUA SECTOR:

POSITION:
South

ELEMENT:
Fire

SEASON:
Summer

COLOR:
Red

TRIGRAM:
Li

Your Recognition and Fame space is in the south of each room in your home. This is a lovely area, as it is all about how people see you: your talents and achievements, how charismatic you are, how your friends view your personality, and how you attain recognition for the work you do and become a star in your chosen field. It is about your own self-development, how you tap into your spirituality and connect to your inner self to find out who you really are and what you want to attain in your life. This area also deals with your zest for getting the most out of each day. Your special "star" space, which projects your future to the world, can be created on a table or shelf in the living room, dining room, study, or bedroom.

Boosting your Recognition and Fame space

Before you start looking at symbols and energizers to put in place in your southern area, check what you already have positioned there. Remember that

this space is all about your current status—who you are and who you are aspiring to be—so if you have left old graduation pictures or diplomas here, you are linking yourself too much to your past as a student. Throw out cards from people you no longer see or with whom you have fallen out, and discard any photographs of you in which you look unhappy, dejected, or miserable. Don't keep any job-rejection letters here as these tarnish your image and will unsettle your present work potential. If you are a writer, singer, or actor, make sure that no bad reviews of your books, concerts, films, or plays are kept here, as they will give out the message that you are never going to be a success at what you do. Take out any dying plants

LEFT For some people fame is about becoming a celebrity in their chosen field and constantly being on show and in the public eye.

✦ Framed diplomas of your chosen profession will boost your fame.

Recognition and Fame activators

To inspire the fame that you deserve, put some of these pieces in the southern space of the living room or other chosen room:

✦ Red flowers or red flowering plants will liven up the area as Wood feeds Fire in the element cycle.

✦ Framed diplomas of your chosen profession will boost your fame.

✦ A red lamp or candles will increase the existing Fire energy.

✦ Star symbols, star cards, or a framed picture with a star pattern denotes the star quality you are seeking.

✦ Include a model or image of something you desire such as an exotic trip, a villa abroad, a car, or a boat so that you can look at it on a regular basis.

or flowers, as they will bring stagnancy to this space rather than inspiring energy. Similarly, old sports equipment that you no longer use or a discarded musical instrument that you have given up playing will keep you tied to the person you have left behind. If your job is just not working out, seek out a position that better suits your aims and goals. Also let go of any restrictions from childhood. Remember that with positive thinking you can achieve anything you want.

Choosing inspirational symbols and energizers such as bright lights, framed diplomas, and red flowers will let your star quality really shine and show everyone how you are going to make your mark on the world.

MARRIAGE AND ROMANTIC HAPPINESS

PA KUA SECTOR:

POSITION:
Southwest

ELEMENT:
Strong Earth

SEASON:
Late summer

COLOR:
Yellow or beige

TRIGRAM:
K'un

Your Marriage and Romantic Happiness space sits in the southwest corner of each room in your home. This area is associated with love and enduring relationships. It is the place of romance where new liaisons can be enticed into your life. Passion and sexuality are strong emotions here—this is the place where you open up your heart to your special lover and the person with whom you hope to spend the rest of your life. It is about real togetherness, a true partnership, where your mind and emotions meet and blend into one.

A romantic shrine, shelf, or table is especially appropriate in the bedroom; in fact, if you want to, you can turn the whole room into a passionate boudoir to show that you mean business. Alternatively, you can place it in the southwestern space of your living room or dining room to lift the loving vibrations and attract that desired partner.

✦ A rose quartz crystal is the ultimate lover's stone.

ABOVE Your Marriage and Romantic Happiness space is all about togetherness, love, and long-term relationships. It is about the joining of two minds as well as physical union.

Boosting your Marriage and Romantic Happiness space

Before you spice up your chosen Marriage and Romantic Happiness space, walk around the area and see what you have there. If you have never really let go of a past partner, you may still be displaying photographs of them or hoarding old love letters here that will just keep you in their energy and not allow in a new, exciting lover. This is an area of enduring romance, so pictures

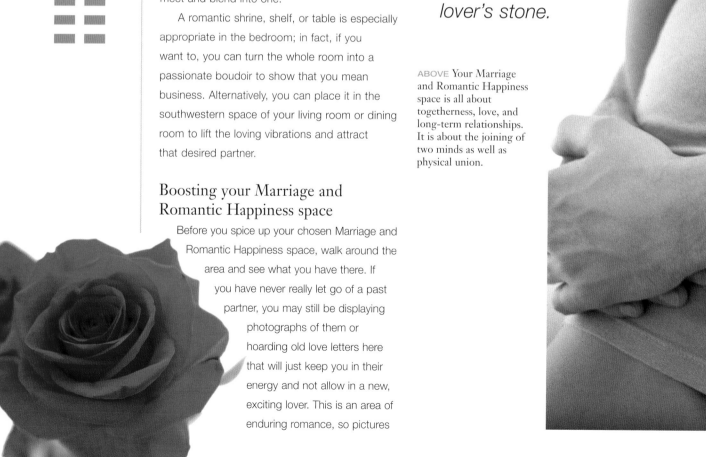

Marriage and Romantic Happiness activators

To be a magnet for that desired lover or to keep the magic in your existing relationship, place some of the following in the southwestern space of your bedroom, living room, or other chosen room:

✦ Red or pink candles will fire up the energy here as Fire feeds Earth in the element cycle.

✦ A rose quartz crystal is the ultimate lover's stone and gives out wonderful romantic vibrations.

✦ Two glass hearts will show the pairing of your heart with that of your partner and encourage a loving partnership.

✦ A paired or entwined statue or a photograph of a loving couple spells out love and passion.

✦ Draw up a list of qualities you seek in a lover, and make sure you are specific about the partner you desire, as you will get what you ask for. Put the list in a special box under your rose quartz crystal.

of strong single women or sad, depressed-looking couples have no place here as they say you either prefer to be alone or no longer want a relationship. Also get rid of any pictures of doomed lovers, such as Romeo and Juliet. Damaged or broken statues of lovers and chipped heart images will doom your relationship if they are not quickly removed. Discard old address books containing ex-lovers' telephone numbers, and throw away any cherished Valentine's Day cards if you truly want a new, desirable partner.

A rose quartz crystal, red or pink candles, and a statue of a loving couple are just some of the charming symbols and energizers that you can put here to attract that desired dream lover or to preserve and strengthen an enduring marriage or long-term relationship.

CHILDREN AND PROJECTS

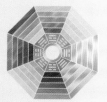

POSITION:
West

ELEMENT:
Small Metal

SEASON:
Autumn

COLOR:
**White
(also metallic,
gold, and silver)**

TRIGRAM:
Tui

Your Children and Projects space is sited in the west of each room of your home. This is an area that is associated with female energies, procreation, and female fertility. It is about the children that you desire to have soon or it can involve nurturing and fostering the growth of the precious ones you already have. Hopes for a bright future exist here and the new family that is so longed for. However, the Children and Projects area is not only about physical offspring, it is also about your creative juices, how you can develop new exciting projects from nothing. Here you can start a new business project, initiate a passion for a new hobby, or fulfill a dream undertaking such as buying a villa abroad. Place fertility symbols on a shelf or table in the west space of a bedroom or living room, and project details in the west space of the living room or dining room.

Boosting your Children and Projects space

Before you start encouraging more fertility, physically or mentally, into your Children and Projects area, appraise what you have left there.

✦ *A statue of a couple with a child gives out the message that you really want a family.*

Children and Projects activators

To boost your fertility or to give good "vibes" to a treasured project, put some of these items in the western space of your bedroom, living room, or dining room:

✦ A piece of carnelian crystal will help to increase your creativity or stimulate your passion in the bedroom.

✦ A statue of a couple with a child gives out the message that you really want a family.

✦ Paperwork or pictures relating to a new business plan, new hobby details, an exciting project idea, or a dream home will fuel them with positive energies.

✦ Fertility symbols such as baby booties, a pregnancy-testing kit, a child image, and a baby book can be positioned here.

✦ Ceramic and terra-cotta figurines and bowls will lift the energies here as Earth feeds Metal in the element cycle.

ABOVE LEFT, LEFT, AND BELOW Your space in the west is not only about children but is associated with your creative talents. It is about your ability to get involved with new projects, to design, write wonderful music, make beautiful beaded objects, or create superb paintings.

Any junk under the bed could affect your fertility, your desire for a baby, and your creative juices, so clear it out immediately. Bad school report cards, unfinished essays or abandoned science projects here can pull down your child's current performance at school. Disturbed or violent paintings and broken toys or electronic equipment should be removed from this space in your child's bedroom. Failed or discarded business projects should also be taken out of this space as they will affect the viability of any new ones on which you are embarking. Any other abandoned projects such as a half-finished novel, a rejected business plan, or discarded material relating to an old hobby can stop you from starting fulfilling new adventures.

Placing a statue of a couple with a child, a stimulating crystal, and some ceramics (see activators, above) in this space will help to bring in that desired child or activate that new dream project.

MENTORS AND NETWORKING

POSITION:
Northwest

ELEMENT:
Strong Metal

SEASON:
Autumn

COLOR:
**White
(also metallic,
gold, and silver)**

TRIGRAM:
Chien

*✦ A piece
of rutilated
quartz
crystal will
increase
your
spiritual
growth.*

Your Mentors and Networking space is located in the northwest of each room in your home. This area is related to the strong authority figures, leaders, or inspirational people who are important in your life and who will help to mold your as yet unknown future. A mentor can also be interpreted as a god figure or a spiritual leader, such as Jesus Christ, Buddha, angels, or the Hindu or Chinese gods who offer guidance whenever you need them throughout your life.

On a lesser level, the Mentors and Networking space is about the helpful people who assist in the smooth day-to-day running of your life: the plumbers, electricians, builders, decorators, relative and friends helping you with the school carpool, and babysitters. It is about keeping and making new contacts and friends and extending your social circle to bring in more fulfillment and happiness.

An altar to the gods with incense and candles can be placed in the northwest of a bedroom or living room, while a bulletin board, a networking phone book, and any other accessories you use for communication are better positioned in a kitchen or in a living area.

Boosting your Mentors and Networking space

Before you start meditating at your altar or working on improving your circle of useful contacts, take a careful look around the Mentors and Networking area in your home and see what you have deposited there. Search for any broken or damaged statues of spiritual leaders or gods as these can inhibit your spiritual growth and progression. Old address books, discarded business cards of trades people, and old contact lists or unused bulletin boards, for example, will

Mentors and Networking activators

To send out the right networking pulsations or to seek inspired help from your mentor, add some of the following to the northwestern space of your bedroom, living room or kitchen:

✦ Include a gold laughing Buddha or a ceramic Buddha or other spiritual leader or god to increase your luck and spiritual guidance. Alternatively, put a photo of your spiritual leader in a metal frame to support the energies here.

✦ A six-rod metal wind chime will activate your networking skills.

✦ Calendars, day planners, address books, personal organizers, and BlackBerries placed here will bring in more positive contacts.

✦ A piece of rutilated quartz crystal will increase your spiritual growth.

✦ Ceramic pots and figurines will boost the energy here as Earth feeds Metal in the Productive element cycle.

just keep you in the past and stop you from moving forward with your networking.

On the work front, take out any negative appraisals or critical correspondence with colleagues that will hamper your work interaction or how you relate to your boss.

Complaining letters or depressed cards from friends or relatives have no place in this space, as they will not foster meeting new friends and acquaintances. The aim is to leave behind people who are no longer part of your life so that you allow new ones in who relate to your current image and position.

A ceramic mentor statue, a six-rod metal wind chime, and calendars or day planners placed here (see activators, above right) will help start the jungle drums, encouraging more contacts into your life plus more guidance and help from your chosen mentors.

ABOVE A charismatic leader, such as South Africa's Nelson Mandela, is one of the mentors who have changed the future of a nation.

RIGHT Buddhist leader the Dalai Lama still leads his people, giving them spiritual guidance, despite being in exile in the West.

The Best Feng Shui Cures and Enhancements

Enhancements can be used to boost the energy in all eight life aspirational areas of the Pa Kua (see pages 32–47). For example, you can place a running water feature in your Wealth and Prosperity space to increase your funds or a candle or lamp in your Recognition and Fame space to stimulate your star quality.

Cures can be positioned around the home to offset negative energy being directed at the building, to slow down fast energy flow, or to neutralize sha chi (negative energy) coming off sharp corners or columns. Houseplants absorb pollutants in the atmosphere and can soak up electromagnetic energy emitted by televisions, stereo systems, and computers. By boosting the flow of chi in some areas and balancing out negative areas with the right cure you will harmonize your home and notice the positive uplift in the atmosphere.

How do they work?

Enhancements and cures work in various ways to lift energy or smooth out harsh chi that may be negatively affecting you and your family.

Houseplants: These are versatile cures for when you have sha chi in your home. They are also very yang and great energizers. (See page 50.)

RIGHT Candles give out a soft, warm glow that creates intimacy in the bedroom or living room. Their yang presence will also help stimulate lively conversation at a dinner party.

Water features or aquariums: Both of these activate chi flow, and when placed in the Wealth corner they encourage a good flow of money into your life. (See page 51.)

Lights and candles: These raise the yang energy in stagnant or dark areas and can ignite the Recognition and Fame area. (See pages 52–3.)

Crystals: These are vital for raising energy levels in different parts of the home. They are also great healers and can offset negativity or give protection when needed. Although lead-faceted hanging crystals are not actual crystals, they are essential feng shui tools to activate chi flow or to ward off cutting chi from obstacles. (See pages 53–54.)

Wind chimes: The lovely sound of wind chimes activates chi flow or helps to slow it down if it is moving too fast. They are ideal for a hallway in which the staircase is directly opposite the door and energy is consequently moving too fast. (See page 53.)

Mirrors: Powerful energizers, mirrors can double the energy of a space and are also good at expanding narrow spaces. They should be used with caution in the bedroom, however, as they are too energetic for this yin space. Use Pa Kua mirrors only outside the home to ward off sha energy from buildings, as they are too strong to use inside. (See page 55.)

ABOVE Crystals are wonderful energizers and cures that can be used in the home to balance the atmosphere.

ABOVE Hanging a wind chime in a living room will stimulate the energy flow and make the room feel bright and airy.

ABOVE Bamboo flutes are great cures for ceiling beams, as they are believed to dissipate the bad chi that comes off the beams.

Bamboo flutes: These can offset the cutting chi that comes from ceiling beams. Tie two bamboo flutes onto the offending beam with red thread to resolve the problem. (In Cantonese "flutes" means "disappear," which explains their derivation.)

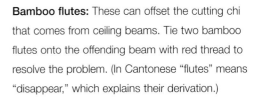

TOP LEFT The Black Tortoise is the celestial guardian that symbolizes the north or the back area of your home. TOP RIGHT The White Tiger represents the lower hills on the right or in the west. BOTTOM LEFT The auspicious Green Dragon is located in the east or is seen as the higher hills on the left. BOTTOM RIGHT The lucky Red Phoenix links to the space in front of your home or to the south area.

The Celestial Guardians: These four animal spirits are very protective and represent aspects of the landscape surrounding your home.

The Black Tortoise: Symbolizing hills or distant mountains behind the home, a Black Tortoise image placed in the north or at the back of the home will improve your lifestyle and increase your prosperity.

The Green Dragon: Representing the slightly higher hills on the left (as you look out of your front door), a Green Dragon image placed here or in the east will bring material success and good fortune.

The White Tiger: Depicting the slightly lower hills on your home's right (as you look out of your front door), a White Tiger image sited here or in the west will act as your home's protective guardian.

The Red Phoenix: Portraying the space and low land in front of your home, an image of the Red Phoenix here or in the south should bring good luck and new opportunities.

Houseplants

Healthy green plants with round or succulent leaves are vital feng shui enhancements for different parts of the home. They give out bracing oxygen as part of their growing process, making the atmosphere feel more vital. Many familiar houseplants (including the gerbera and the rubber plant) are excellent at absorbing and neutralizing common indoor pollutants in the air. As energizers they can be placed in dark, stagnant corners to increase the energy flow there. They are ideal in kitchens to increase the yang energy, but take care not to position them too close to the stove—as part of the Wood element that feeds Fire in the element cycle, they may cause the stove to overheat. In the sluggish atmosphere of bathrooms, they help to reduce humidity and raise the existing chi levels.

As a cure, houseplants can obscure sharp angles to prevent cutting chi from coming off corners, pillars, or furniture. They can also be placed in halls to slow down the energy flow

between two doors or to slow its progression up the stairs when the front door is opposite a staircase. Placing houseplants near electrical equipment will help to counterbalance the effects of the electromagnetic fields (EMFs) that they emit.

A jade plant (*Crassula argentea*), also called a money tree, can help to increase your fortunes when you put it in your Wealth and Prosperity space in the southeast of your rooms. Watch how it grows, as it is supposed to mirror your fortunes. Peace lilies (*Spathiphyllum wallisii*), peperomias, and goosefoot plants (*Syngonium podophyllum*) help soak up EMFs when placed next to televisions and computers.

To enhance the Wood element, site plants in the east, your Family and Health space, and in the southeast, your Wealth and Prosperity area. They can also boost the energy in your Recognition and Fame space in the south as Wood feeds Fire in the element cycle.

The only plants not to use in the home are ones with long spiky leaves as these can give off sha chi, so always choose varieties with round leaves.

ABOVE Healthy plants with rounded leaves such as the peace lily lift the energy in living rooms and kitchens.

LEFT A jade plant can boost your finances if you place it in the southeast of a room (but not the bedroom).

Water features

The wonderful trickling sound of running water is very soothing mentally and emotionally. Water is also a great cleanser and can revive a flagging spirit. Running water is believed to activate chi and bring prosperity into your life, so having an indoor water feature can be very beneficial.

An aquarium can be auspicious as the fish create a dynamic flow of chi. Choose an odd number of lively goldfish, such as three or nine which are both considered to be lucky, and include one that is black to absorb negativity. The oxygenated water in the aquarium and the movement of the fish stimulate the chi in the water. Place in the southeast (your Wealth and Prosperity corner) as Water feeds Wood in the element cycle. You can also place it in the north (your Career corner) to support the existing Water energies there. Alternatively, you could use a small water fountain, a flowing water feature, or even a pitcher of still water in this space.

Water features should never be positioned in a bedroom, as they are too strong. This is because the bedroom is considered to be the Earth element and Water overwhelms Earth in the Clashing cycle. Too much water here is thought to encourage relationship problems. Outdoors, siting a small pond or fountain to the left of the front door (as you look out) will bring good chi into your home. Fountains can also be used to dissipate any cutting chi that is hitting your home from the corners of buildings or from a straight road opposite, for example. Be sure always to keep the water fresh outside to prevent stagnancy.

ABOVE The Pa Kua is an important feng shui tool to use to find out where all your life aspirational spaces are situated in your home.

ABOVE A goldfish bowl or aquarium can be placed in the southeast of a room (but not the bedroom) to stimulate chi and encourage a good flow of money. RIGHT A fountain can encourage good chi into the home if it is sited outside the home on the left-hand side.

Lights and candles

Both lights and candles link to the Fire element and can bring positive yang energy into the rooms of your home. Ambient, or background, lighting can fill a room with soft, warm light; task lighting helps you read or work; and accent lighting can be used to highlight pictures, *objets*, collections, or striking houseplants.

Lighting affects moods—when it is soft it is relaxing, while bright, strong light stimulates creativity. Careful planning of your home's lighting will produce a feeling of balance and harmony.

Wherever possible, choose floor and table lamps in shapes that will match the element of the area where they are being placed. For example, tall, straight lamps are most appropriate to the east and southeast areas, which relate to the element Wood. Rounded, oval or dome-shaped lamps are best in the west and north-west, the areas that link to Metal. Square or rectangular lamps can go in the southwest and northeast areas, which are associated with Earth. Flowing or irregular-shaped lamps are suited to the north as they relate to the Water element.

BELOW Background lighting, such as that provided by lamps, creates a warm light that can lift the energy in dark corners or spaces.

Candles give out a soft glow and create an aura of romance in a bedroom or for an intimate dinner. They create tranquility around a home altar used for meditation, and scattered around a living room or placed in a fireplace they induce a calm ambience. Put candles around a bath or in sconces on the bathroom wall to promote deep relaxation. Their yang presence will also counteract the sluggish energy that exists in a bathroom.

Wind chimes

The soft tinkle of wind chimes is always a pleasant sound to hear as they gently move in the breeze. In ancient China wind chimes were hung up to ward off lost spirits, but today their influence is much more positive in the home. When a five-rod metal wind chime is hung outside the home, it can filter or break up sha chi aimed at the front door. When placed just inside the door, a wind chime's vibrant sound will slow down the fast energy flow resulting from a staircase being opposite the door. Wind chimes are also marvelous energizers as their sound stimulates the flow of chi.

If you want to use a wind chime as an energizer, first check the room's direction and element so that you can choose the right type of wind chime—but always use a five-rod chime to match the five elements. Place metal wind chimes in the west and northwest (Metal) and in the north (Water is fed by Metal in the element cycle). Ceramic wind chimes are best in the southwest and northeast (Earth), while wooden wind chimes suit the east and southeast (Wood) and the south (Fire is fed by Wood in the element cycle).

Crystals

Formed millions of years ago, crystals are found in many parts of the world. They give out and strengthen electromagnetic vibrations, which can lift the energy in the home or change or transmute any negativity encountered. You can use both rough and polished crystals in the home, as the healing energy will be just the same.

In feng shui a number of crystals particularly benefit the home (see page 54). Some combinations can boost your finances in your Wealth corner, entice in a new romantic relationship, or enhance the love in an existing one. Others can protect the home from difficult neighbors or bring in joy or good luck. Natural quartz is one of the most versatile crystals as it energizes a room and cures any stagnancy or negative energy. Spherical lead-faceted crystals, despite the fact that they are not real crystals, can be hung in windows to offset cutting chi and lift the energetics in a dull room.

ABOVE Metal wind chimes should be placed in the west or northwest when you want to boost the energy of the room.

The best feng shui crystals

These are the best feng shui crystals to alter the energy in your home and produce the harmony you seek:

Crystal	Place and use
AMETHYST AND CITRINE 	Amethyst promotes feelings of love and spiritual wisdom while citrine increases joy, optimism, and intuition. The combination of these crystals can be placed in the southwest of your rooms (except bathrooms and toilets), your Marriage space, to bring joy and love into a new or existing relationship.
AVENTURINE, CITRINE, AND ROSE QUARTZ 	Aventurine is the gambler's talisman, an all-round good luck stone. Rose quartz is a loving crystal that attracts success. When matched with citrine (see above) they give out the right vibrations to attract financial success to your Wealth space in the southeast of your rooms.
HEMATITE 	A very yang crystal that dissolves negativity and prevents bad energies or unwanted people from entering the home. Place it on a windowsill or under the outside doormat.
JADE 	Jade attracts joy, luck, and abundance for all the family. Glue a piece inside or under your mailbox.
SPHERICAL LEAD-FACETED CRYSTAL 	Hang a ¾–1¼in/20–30mm spherical lead-faceted crystal in a window to offset the cutting chi from lampposts, single trees, or jutting corners from buildings. Also hang one between two windows to slow down energy, or in a room to liven up the energy.
NATURAL QUARTZ	The most profound healing crystal, rose quartz can amplify energy and get rid of negativity in the home. Use it in spaces where the energy is low. Glue small pieces at both ends of a ceiling beam to offset the sha chi and place one on the desk in your study to improve focus and concentration.
ROSE QUARTZ 	A crystal that gives out unconditional love. It relates to the heart chakra and love relationships. Use it as part of the Wealth combination above and put it by the bed to encourage romance and loving feelings.

LEFT Mirrors are potent energizers that should not be misused. Place them opposite a pleasant view or in the hallway, for example, to expand the space.

ABOVE A small mirror, such as the one above, is ideal to use in the bedroom where the use of mirrors should be kept to the minimum.

Mirrors

Through the ages mirrors were thought to have magical powers, and only pharaohs, kings, and shamans were allowed to have them. They are great expanders of energy, and when placed in a narrow hallway a flat mirror will brighten the area and create the illusion of more space. Pa Kua mirrors are very powerful and protective but should only be hung up outside the home to deflect negative energy back to its source. Be careful how you position them as you may send bad energy to a good neighbor by mistake.

Symbolically, mirrors can also double energy. If you place one opposite a dining table, for example, it will appear to double the amount of food on the table, which is believed to increase the prosperity of the family. Do not hang one opposite your desk, however, as you will double your existing workload. Putting a mirror on your powder-room door, if it is opposite the front door, will make it "disappear." Several mirrors can also bring back "missing" corners of rooms. If your Wealth area is missing in the living room, for example, put two mirrors facing inward on one wall of the L-shape to reinstate it.

WHAT NOT TO DO

Mirrors are so powerful that you need to take care when using them. Bear in mind the following warnings:

+ Never position mirrors facing each other, as they will bounce chi back and forth.

+ A mirror opposite a front door will just send the energy straight out again.

+ Throw out a cracked or discolored mirror as it will literally tarnish your image.

+ Never put up a mirror or have mirror doors opposite your bed as this can cause restlessness, insomnia, and possibly relationship problems.

+ Avoid using mirror tiles as they break up your image and can also cause fragmentation in your life.

+ Dusty mirrors will distort the energetics, so always keep them sparkling clean.

The Pa Kua

The feng shui consultant's main diagnostic tool is the yang Pa Kua, which has what is known as the Later Heaven arrangement of the eight sacred emblems known as trigrams. An octagonal figure, the Pa Kua corresponds to the four cardinal points of the compass and its four intercardinal points.

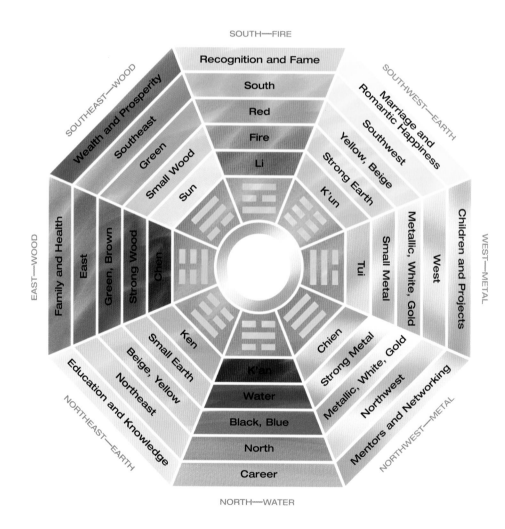

LEFT The Pa Kua is the main diagnostic tool of the feng shui consultant. It has eight segments and is divided into six rings, relating to the trigram and its name, along with the element, color, direction, and life aspirational space.

"Pa" means "eight" and "kua" means "trigram." Each of the eight trigrams contained in the Pa Kua consists of a set of broken (yin) and/or unbroken (yang) lines that make up the 64 hexagrams in the ancient Chinese book the *I Ching*, or Book of Changes. The hexagrams in the *I Ching* are believed to have deep meanings and profound interpretations, holding the mysteries of the universe. In both Pa Kua arrangements—yin, or Early Heaven, and yang, or Later Heaven—south is at the top and north at the bottom, which corresponds to the Chinese compass.

The yin Pa Kua arrangement was used for tombs and burial grounds and was thought to make this Pa Kua very protective. Today it is used only in Pa Kua mirrors for deflecting energy outside the home. Representing a balance of opposing elements, it placed the *chien* trigram in the south and the *k'un* trigram in the north.

The yang Pa Kua represents the nature of cyclical change. In it, the *li* trigram is in the south and the *k'an* trigram in the north.

When you are mapping out your home you can place the yang Pa Kua over the whole house or apartment, or over each room, which is my personal preference.

How it is used

The Pa Kua has six rings. The inner ring shows the potent trigrams, and the second ring has the Chinese name of the trigram. The third ring relates to the five elements (see page 20): Wood, Metal, and Earth have two directions while Water and Fire have one. The fourth ring shows the color of the element: Fire is red, Earth is yellow or beige, Metal is white, Water is blue or black, and Wood is green. The fifth ring depicts the compass directions, which you can align with your room's orientation (see page 58) on all your plans. The sixth ring shows the life aspirations (see page 32): the south is Recognition and Fame, the southwest

is Marriage and Romantic Happiness, the west is Children and Projects, the northwest is Mentors and Networking, the north is Career, the northeast is Education and Knowledge, the east is Family and Health, and the southeast is Wealth and Prosperity.

The life aspirational spaces are very important in the home as they can be boosted with element enhancements and other symbols to increase your luck, to help your love life progress, to improve your career prospects, or to bring in that longed-for child or desired project.

BELOW Each of the rings of the Pa Kua is linked to a different aspect of the area to which it relates.

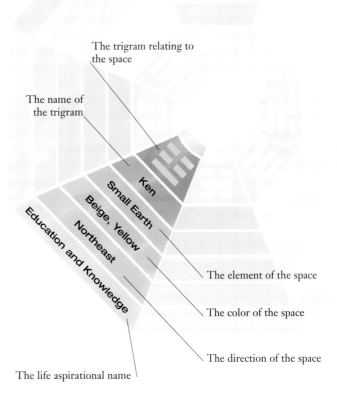

The trigram relating to the space

The name of the trigram

Ken

Small Earth

Beige, Yellow

Northeast

Education and Knowledge

The element of the space

The color of the space

The direction of the space

The life aspirational name

How to Draw Plans
of Your Home

One of the first tasks you need to undertake when you are using feng shui is to map out your home. Start by taking a compass orientation of each room and your front door to find out from what direction the chi or energy is entering the room. You do not need to spend a lot of money on a compass—a basic orienteering style can be purchased from a sports or camping equipment store.

Taking compass readings

With your compass in your hand, open your front door and stand in the doorway looking out. Turn your compass until the main pointer (which is normally red) aligns with north. If this pointer is facing directly into the home, then the energy is entering from the south, normally shown by the white part of the pointer. Write down this direction and then go around all the rooms in your home and note down their orientations in the same way. Always stand on the threshold of the doorway looking out when you are taking a reading, as you want to know the direction that the energy enters the room, not the way it faces.

If a reading seems unstable, step back further into the room, as the compass can be affected by pipework, steel beams, or other metal supports.

Drawing up your plans

Now that you have taken your readings and learned about the Pa Kua (see page 56) you can start to draw up your room plans. To do this you will need some graph paper and a Pa Kua outline traced to scale from page 56.

ABOVE Turn the compass until the red pointer aligns with north so that you can see the direction that the energy is coming from.

Face outward to take the reading—the compass will show you the direction of energy coming into the room.

Stand in the doorway of the room with your back to the door in order to take your compass reading.

How to draw up a Pa Kua room plan

1 Draw up the square or rectangular shape of the room. With a ballpoint pen, draw in the doorway on the left, right, or middle of the grid, leaving some wall space on the left if there is some.

2 In pencil, mark the halfway points on the bottom horizontal line and the right-hand vertical line. Now draw in vertical and horizontal lines that meet in the middle.

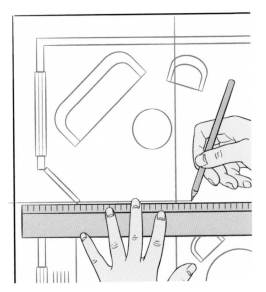

3 Place the middle of your traced Pa Kua on this center point. Using a pin, swivel the tracing around until the left, right, or middle doorway matches the room's direction.

4 Mark all the points of the Pa Kua's sections —for example, south, Recognition and Fame—and draw them in, making the lines longer than the room's shape if necessary, to show your aspirational spaces. Mark in the rest of the outer shape. Now draw in all the lines to the center point.

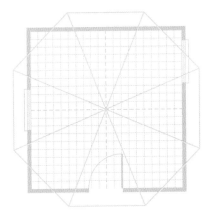

Putting the Pa Kua on a square room

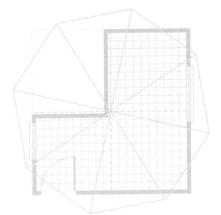

Putting the Pa Kua on an L-shaped room

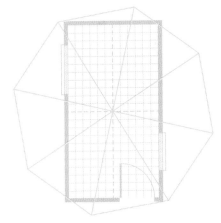

Putting the Pa Kua on a rectangular room

Vertical rectangular rooms are drawn up in the same way. With an odd-shaped room, such as an L-shape, you will have one or two spaces of the Pa Kua missing. To find out what these are, draw up the room's shape on your graph paper. Again mark your halfway points on the bottom and right vertical line and then draw in your horizontal and vertical lines to meet in the middle. Fill in the missing segment of the room with a dotted line in pencil, then place your Pa Kua on the middle point and move it around to match the door's orientation to see what spaces are missing—normally 1½ spaces. To reinstate these spaces symbolically, fix mirrors to one of the walls of the L-shaped corner.

Clearing Out Your Junk

According to Chinese philosophy, the invisible life force called chi flows through everything. Manipulating and balancing this flow of electromagnetic energy is the major part of feng shui practice. When chi flows around the home freely, the atmosphere is bright, vibrant, and uplifting to all the inhabitants.

Moving in a snakelike fashion, chi enters the home through the front door and exits through the back door and windows, where more chi enters and then exits through the front door. Because it needs a positive transit through the home, any piles of clutter or other blockages will slow it down, making it sluggish and lethargic. Unfortunately, once one pile of clutter appears, another seems to quickly follow. Clutter smells musty and stagnant, particularly if it has been left for a long time or is accumulating in dark corners.

If you have piles of clutter in your hallway by the front door or in the porch, you are blocking the "mouth" of the home because that is where chi enters. This will make the chi struggle to move around the home, which will have a detrimental effect on the family. People will start to feel confused, indecisive, or stuck in a rut.

Possessions have energy

Possessions that you love every time you look at them and that you use regularly give off a vibrant energy that promotes good chi flow and inspires a joyful ambience. However, if you are neglecting your home and filling it with junk or items that are broken or don't work, their negative emissions will pull you down and make you feel depressed.

BELOW Keeping possessions or plants that you love on your shelves will fill the room with loving and uplifting vibrations. Limit them to the few that are your favorites, for maximum impact.

Throwing out or giving away articles that no longer have any meaning for you will lift your spirits and emotions, improve your mental attitude, and make you feel better physically as the burden is removed.

What is the definition of clutter?

Clutter is any piece of clothing or other possession that you no longer like, use, or wear. It is something broken that you are not going to repair. The problem with most of us is that we hang on to items we own because we form such a strong emotional attachment to them, especially if they have been given to us by a good friend or a loved relative. We even seem to keep unwanted or peculiar bits and pieces that we inherited because they make us think of the person who owned them every time we look at them. If your home is more like a mausoleum, you will stay stuck in the past and will not allow new events, opportunities, or people into your life. Giving away or throwing out what is not needed is liberating and will truly transform your life.

Your home is supposed to mirror you, so if it is an utter mess, what on earth is going on inside you? Clutter can be used as a protective barrier in the home and may sometimes be mirrored by the person who lives there being a bit overweight. Letting go of any possessions that have been in the home for a long time is a painful process, so don't underestimate this—take it slowly. By clearing out just one drawer or cupboard a day you will release energy, and in no time at all you will see how it has transformed your life.

Be positive about why you are having a clear-out—you may want to have friends to stay in your cluttered spare room or perhaps you want to turn it into a study. Write down your long-term aims and see how good you feel when you start achieving them.

ABOVE Overloading your attic with unwanted junk or items from your childhood will create a black, stagnant cloud that is always hanging over you.

RIGHT Giving away or getting rid of old shoes that you no longer wear is liberating and will make you feel so much better.

STARTING THE CLEARING-OUT PROCESS

When you start to clear out your clutter, don't feel that you have to throw out everything. It is perfectly acceptable to keep some possessions that remind you of happy times in the past, provided that when you look at them you get a good feeling.

However, holding on to too many will keep you tied to the past and will not let you progress in your life. In fact, once you have let go of old possessions, you often don't miss them at all, and if you have given them to a thrift shop you will have the added benefit of knowing you have helped other people. Store cherished mementos from your childhood, your children's school days or special holidays in a nice box that you can get out from time to time when you are feeling sentimental.

Tackling clutter

Start by tackling your clutter on a day when you feel alert and mentally and emotionally refreshed. Go around each room, drawing a rough plan of it and marking in where the piles of junk are. Also quickly check your Pa Kua plans (see pages 58–59) to see if any junk is affecting your life aspirational spaces. If you haven't drawn up the plans yet, mark out the spaces with the Pa Kua to see if you have dumped any unwanted goods in your Family space, which would explain recent arguments. Or you may have left broken items in your Marriage space and wondered why communication with your partner had been so bad recently.

Do a maximum of three hours' clearing at a time. If you get too emotional, limit it to half an hour and praise yourself for what you have achieved. A good way to sort out clutter is to use the five-bag system. Get five strong garbage bags (and several spares). Label them as shown opposite.

BELOW Everyday junk, such as books and general paperwork, can gather into clutter mountains. Recycle unwanted material or store what you do want in accessible units for easy reference.

Clear your clutter with the five-bag system

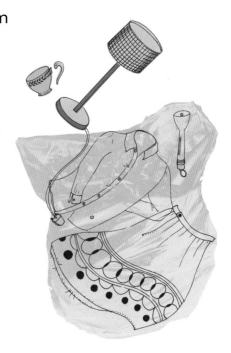

1 **Junk** (this is everything that you want to go to the dump)

2 **Charity or friends** (items that you no longer like but that thrift shops or friends might want)

3 **Things to repair or alter** (articles that you still want to keep but that need mending)

4 **Things to sort and move** (those items that ought to be stored somewhere else)

5 **Transitional items** (possessions you just can't seem to let go). Keep this bag for six months in the attic or in a cupboard. If you miss the contents, get them out again, otherwise pass them on at the end of the six months.

Recycling

You will probably need an extra bag for recycling paper, particularly if you have a home office. You may not use all the bags but label them anyway and see how quickly they fill up.

Clothing

Be strict with yourself about clothes. Most of us wear no more than about 20 percent of our wardrobes. Keep only the things that you really love and that suit you and your present image. If you are struggling to let clothes go, bring in a friend as an arbiter. Try everything on in front of them and get rid of any they dislike or think are unflattering.

CLUTTER DANGER ZONES

Clutter in any part of the home slows down energy flow and creates chaos that affects all the family, but when it is stored in certain areas it can have a particularly detrimental effect.

The doorway and entry hall

The front door and entry hall are where chi enters your home, and it is here that you welcome in guests, friends, and relatives, so the first impression of this area is very important. It needs to be a bright, well-lit space that is pleasant and inviting. If you or your family uses it as a dumping ground and it is full of abandoned sports gear, shoes and boots, school bags, children's toys, old newspapers, or junk mail, you are stopping the energy in its tracks and making your life much more of a struggle.

Solution: Recycle all the junk mail, newspapers, and cardboard. Ask all the family to stow their items in their rooms. In the coat closet or by the door, install a large shoe rack where everybody can leave their shoes and boots. Get rid of any unclaimed items that are not being used. Now see how much better you feel with a clear energy flow.

The attic

This is the area where everything from our past gets stored. Unwanted articles are also placed up here. Many clients have said to me, "But surely if it is stored in the attic it won't affect me." I am afraid this is untrue. If you are storing too much in the attic and can never find anything when you go up there, it is just like a black cloud that is constantly hanging over you and slowing all the family's progress in life.

LEFT Filling up your entry hall with clutter will inhibit chi from entering your home as well as creating a negative impression for visiting friends and family.

Solution: Have a big clear-out and get rid of anything you really do not need—feel what a relief that is. Now plan your storage well. Put up shelves if you need to store paints, tools, children's games, old school textbooks or out-of-date bank statements and tax returns in boxes that are well labeled. Hang ski clothes or rarely used coats and jackets on rails in protective plastic bags.

The basement

If you have a basement, it may be used as a utility room or children's playroom but it is likely also to have become a dumping ground for unwanted junk. This area is supposed to be linked to your subconscious, so if you have allowed your basement to get cluttered, there may be issues from your past that you haven't dealt with or problems you haven't managed to resolve.

BELOW The basement is another area that can become a dumping ground for discarded articles. Plan in good storage cupboards and shelving, and keep only what is used and wanted.

Solution: Have a big clear-out in this room and feel your world lifting and your past fading as you discard

ABOVE Don't store old newspapers by your back door as they will block exiting chi. Instead, keep them in a cupboard for recycling.

all that unnecessary junk. If this is a laundry room, make sure you have big baskets where people can leave their dirty clothes rather than dumping them on the floor. Adequate shelving or cupboards will be useful for detergents and other household products. Try to keep as much off the floor as possible, as energy flow is very slow in basements.

The back door

This is where everything leaves your home; symbolically it is the organ of excretion, so any clutter here is literally blocking up the home, making it constipated. Discarded wine bottles, piles of plastic and paper bags, an overflowing trash can, and half-eaten pet food are often left here, making this area low on positive energy.

Solution: Sense how you are freeing the energy flow as you place cat and dog bowls elsewhere. Keep your wine and other bottles in a recycling box in the backyard. Move the trash can to another space or empty it regularly and keep it clean. Store plastic bags in a bag tidy and pile reusable plastic and paper bags neatly in a cupboard.

SPACE CLEARING THE ATMOSPHERE

Clearing out all your junk can have an amazing effect on you and the atmosphere in your home, but if it has been there a long time, a lingering mustiness and staleness will be left behind that are hard to shift. Space clearing—removing this stagnancy with a cleansing ceremony—will fire up the newly released energy and give your home a new lease on life.

Space clearing is also appropriate when you have first moved into a property, as the energy of the previous occupants is believed to be held in the walls and needs to be released, particularly if they divorced or one partner died while living there. It is also a good idea to do a minor cleanse after an argument, if someone has been ill or if you have had workmen in, disrupting the energy in the home.

Do not attempt to space clear if you are not feeling well or if you are upset emotionally. Avoid it if you are having your period, are pregnant, or have an open cut. Clean your home thoroughly the day before, and have a bath or shower before you start the ceremony, then change into some casual clothes and take off any jewelry you are wearing.

RIGHT Burning incense sticks is a simple way of space clearing your living room after an argument or disagreement. The perfumed smoke will also help to lift your spirits.

Smudging

A Native American tradition, smudging is the most powerful of the cleansing ceremonies. It will remove any energies left by previous occupants and purify the space of any negativity lingering there. Smudging after clearing out clutter will remove mustiness and make the atmosphere feel bright and charged, as though your home had been spring-cleaned.

Smudge sticks are made from tightly bundled dried herbs which release their cleansing properties when lit. Sweetgrass, rosemary, and sage were often used in Native American tribal ceremonies and they are still the main herbs of today's smudge sticks.

How to smudge

1 Before you start, take a few minutes to connect with your inner self and set your intention for clearing the atmosphere in your home. Light your smudge stick. Make sure it is well lit and burning well, and then blow out the flame—have an old plate to hand to catch any fallen ash. Smudge the smoke all around your body to cleanse your aura (your body's energetic field) of any spiritual or emotional negativity.

2 Now go into the first room to purify and walk clockwise around the room from the door. Holding the smudge stick and plate with one hand, use your other hand to waft the smoke into corners where energy can stagnate, around furniture, and up into the ceiling. Keep mentally repeating your intention as you move around the room. Repeat the process in every room of the house, including the entry hall. Open the windows in each room at the end if they are very smoky.

3 When you have finished, extinguish the smudge stick under running water. Cut off the burnt end and store the stick in a plastic bag. A small smudge stick will last for about three sessions and a large one for much longer. If your hair and clothes smell of smoke, have a shower and change your clothes. Smudge again in a month's time to keep the atmosphere positively charged.

ABOVE AND BELOW
There are two varieties of sage smudge sticks: the herb twigs from ordinary sage (above) and the leathery leaves from white sage (below). Both types give out a purifying, gray smoke that deeply cleanses the atmosphere.

Aromatherapy

Essential oils have a delicious smell and are distilled in a natural way from herbs and plants. All the oils retain the life force, spirit, and energy of the herb or plant from which they have been extracted. Some essential oils can relax you or uplift your spirit, and others can also remove negativity or make the atmosphere more vibrant.

Lavender is the perfect oil for general cleansing as it brings chi back to neutral. Lemon, lime, or orange can stimulate the energy in a room, while the best oils for a deep cleanse are juniper, pine, sage, or eucalyptus. Choose an oil with an aroma that you like, as it will linger in the rooms for a while.

How to use essential oils

1 Half-fill a plant-mister bottle with water, add four or five drops of your chosen oil, and shake well. Stand still for a moment, close your eyes and set your intent for the rooms you are purifying.

2 Starting at the entrance of the first room you are cleansing, walk around the room in a clockwise direction spraying all around. Make sure you mist well into dark corners. Work through each room in the same way.

3 To bring vibrancy back into your home, spray each room every day for a week, then once a week for maintenance. Change the oil regularly as the plastic can affect it.

ABOVE Misting a room with an essential oil such as lavender oil will fill the room with a lovely fragrance, dispel negativity, and bring the energy back to neutral.

LEFT You can use different essential oils to space clear a room. Citrus oils will bring in a fresh ambience, while pine or eucalyptus will clear away energy that is left from previous occupants.

Singing bowls

Singing bowls have been in use for at least four thousand years and have been found in India, Nepal, and Japan. The spiritual centre for singing bowls is Tibet but it is thought that the bowls may have originated in a different country. They are used in the East for healing and creating the right atmosphere for meditation.

A traditional bowl is lovingly made from about seven metals, one of which is a precious metal such as gold, silver, or platinum. Bowls can also be made from traditional quartz—these give out a wonderful clear sound but can be quite fragile to use. When you buy a singing bowl try out several different ones until you find a sound that really resounds with you.

The powerful sound a singing bowl emits clears out any bad or stale energies. When you tap or stroke the bowl, the humming sound it emits expands the energy in a room. When you stroke the bowl with a wooden mallet, the humming sound expands in ever-increasing circles, taking away negativity before spiraling back into the middle of the bowl with positive, new energy.

2 Holding the bowl in the flat palm of one hand, take hold of the mallet and start moving it around the inner or outer edge of the bowl. Feel the vibration of the sound building up. Alternatively, just tap the bowl until you hear a clear, strident tone. As you become part of the sound, stroke or tap the bowl faster, feeling any stagnation moving away and a brighter, vital energy replacing it.

ABOVE A singing bowl is a precious sound instrument to use for space clearing. These bowls are lovingly made in the East from around seven metals.

How to use a singing bowl

1 Stand in the middle of the first room you are purifying and, holding your bowl in your hands, set your intent for clearing the energy.

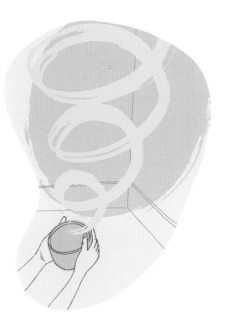

3 After a few minutes stop playing and then work on the other rooms in the same way. When you have finished, thank your bowl for its cleansing work and store it in a special place. Repeat in a week and then play once a month to maintain the vibrancy.

INTERIOR DECORATE WITH FENG SHUI

YOUR HOME IS YOUR NEST, the place where you can relax in your own space and nurture yourself and your family. It needs to be a calm but inspiring environment with a positive energy flow that is not hampered by piles of clutter or other obstructions. Once you understand the basic principles and tools of feng shui, you can apply them to the interior decoration of every room in your home. The right placement of furniture and the skillful use of enhancements or cures can help to improve the atmosphere of each room and boost the level of chi throughout your home. You can discover how to match each room to the color of its element, choose the most effective lighting, and find smooth and flowing furniture styles along with natural fabrics and textures. All will help to create a balanced and harmonious atmosphere.

✦ What can feng shui do for your home?
✦ The front door and hallway
✦ The living room
✦ The dining room
✦ The kitchen
✦ The bathroom
✦ The bedroom
✦ The child's room
✦ The garden

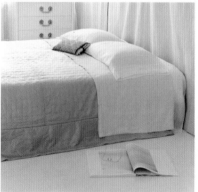

WHAT CAN FENG SHUI DO FOR YOUR HOME?

When you use the techniques of feng shui properly, every aspect of your life will be affected in a positive way.

You will activate beneficial energies that promote the harmony and contentment you are seeking in your environment. Although feng shui principles cannot be tested or proved scientifically, the techniques have scientific precision. It is not a religion but a belief system or philosophy, and its many practical tools have as much use in the modern world as they did thousands of years ago. The main principle of feng shui is to have an active flow of chi through the home, which in turn has a beneficial effect on the occupants and their lives. Enhancements such as crystals and cures such as houseplants further balance the environment so that it is an embracing place to live.

BELOW Allowing spaces around the furniture in your main living space will allow chi to meander around the room freely.

ABOVE Plants are great energizers for the living area. Take care to choose round-leafed plants to avoid cutting chi.

Feng shui can bring you happiness and spiritual and emotional contentment: By loving your home you will love yourself and enjoy your life more. Although financial success is sought by many, it may be your karma not to be wealthy but instead to have a love of life and travel, a family that gets on well together, and a close circle of intimate friends.

Putting feng shui into practice

One of the major ways you can improve your home's energy is to link the colors of each room to the room's element or use the calming or energizing element, depending on the ambience you seek (see pages 20–21). Color has a strong effect on your well-being, and by using this ancient system you can achieve the right ambience in your living space. Putting cures in place to balance any negative chi in the home from pillars, sharp corners, sloping ceilings, or beams will also attract harmony.

The other important way to change your home's energetics is to boost your life aspirational spaces associated with the Pa Kua (see pages 32–47 and 56). Once you have laid the Pa Kua on each room, you will locate the eight special spaces with their potent energies: Recognition and Fame (south), Marriage and Romantic Happiness (southwest), Children and Projects (west), Mentors and Networking (northwest), Career (north), Education and Knowledge (northeast), Family and Health (east), and Wealth and Prosperity (southeast). You can enhance all these spaces so that you and your family have a good chance of success in all areas of your lives, or boost just those that you want to focus on in the next few years, for example Wealth, Career, and Marriage.

Feng shui can help you achieve what you want in your life by making your home work with you to achieve these goals. But you play a big part in this as well. You have to be committed to feng shui and believe in yourself and your ability to gain the best out of your life and your future.

RIGHT It is not good to sleep under the eaves, as it can make you suffer from a feeling of compression. Try to move the bed to another position or place uplighters on either side of it to lift the wall symbolically.

RIGHT Living rooms are normally linked to their calming element color or kept neutral. But if you feel some energizing is needed, add a couple of chairs in the energizing color. Here red chairs have been introduced to an Earth room.

FENG SHUI YOUR HOME
IN 15 STEPS

This step-by-step plan shows you how you can implement feng shui in your home to create balance and harmony. Go through the points as you feng shui each room.

1 Look at the environment surrounding your home to see if anything is negatively affecting you. Watch out for large trees or utility poles directly in front of the home or a straight road that is opposite your front door, as they all send sharp sha or cutting chi at you. Yin places such as churches, doctors' offices, or funeral parlors can also disrupt the yang energy that enters your home. Hanging a five-rod metal wind chime outside your front door or growing shrubs up your front wall or fence can screen off these problem areas. Pa Kua mirrors can also deflect negative influences, but use them with caution as you can inadvertently beam sha chi to your neighbors.

2 Look outside your back door to see how much protection with fencing and walls you have from the neighbors. If you feel vulnerable, create a barrier with tall plants or add trellis so that you can grow climbing plants that will screen any bad energy. Check for satellite dishes or sha energy coming off corners of buildings that are directed at your home. If you have any of these problems, screen them as in step 1 or hang a 1¼in/30mm spherical lead-faceted crystal in the place where the bad energy strikes your home.

3 With your orienteering compass (see page 58) take the direction of the front door of your home and all the rooms in it. Make sure you note down the direction from which the energy enters each room.

4 Using graph paper, sketch out each room and place the Pa Kua (see pages 56–59) on top of each one to find out the position of your life aspirational spaces (see page 32).

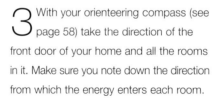

5 Think about the areas in your life that are not working or those that could do with a boost. For example, if your love life is lacking, you will need to enhance the southwest area, linking to the Earth element, with yellow or ceramic items. To energize this space add red accessories, lighting, or candles that associate with the Fire element as Fire feeds Earth in the element cycle (see pages 20–23).

6

7

7 Have a look at each room or area in detail, starting with your front door and entry hall. Make sure you have a curved path leading to your entrance so that chi doesn't rush in too quickly (see page 14). Also cut back any overgrown plants, trees, or shrubs that will restrict people from entering. Check for and remove any junk that has accumulated in the entry hall, as it will restrict the positive chi flow needed here.

6 In an odd or L-shaped room, you are losing one of the spaces of the Pa Kua. If the space is important to you, bring it back in by lining the walls of the opposite wall with mirrors to energetically fill that space.

8

8 Check your kitchen. Make sure that the stove is not visible from the front door, but if it is, create some screening with plants or furniture to obscure it. Insure that your refrigerator, freezer, and sink are not next to the stove as this causes a conflict of the Fire and Water elements. If they are adjacent and can't be moved, put a metal object between them to control the Fire energy.

10

9 Appraise your living room and dining room. Decide whether there are any cluttered areas and whether you have a social arrangement of sofas and chairs. If the dining area is open-plan to the living area, see whether you have demarcated the yang dining area with screens, plants, or bookcases from the calmer, yin living space. Add some pictures of food or fruit to encourage prosperity in a dining room.

10 Look at all the bedrooms in your home. The best position for the bed is diagonally opposite the door. Do not have pictures or shelving over the beds as this can feel oppressive and you will always subconsciously think they are going to fall down on you. Mirrors are very powerful and energetic so if there are any opposite the bed, remove them or cover them at night. Otherwise, they could disrupt this calm environment and bring disturbed sleep or insomnia. Avoid placing beds under sloping ceilings if possible. If they have to be in this position, try tenting

the ceiling or pointing two uplighters toward it to symbolically "lift" this oppressive energy. Do not keep any clutter under the bed as this causes stagnancy and can induce restless sleep or badly affect your love life.

11 In children's bedrooms make sure that the activity area is well separated from the sleeping space or there will be a conflict of yin (sleeping area) and yang (activity area) energies. Ideally, screen off the busy space so that the yin area for sleeping is completely separate. Unplug all electrical equipment at night so that the electromagnetic fields it emits do not disturb sleeping children.

12 Check your bathrooms and powder rooms. If you have a powder room opposite or near the front door, its yin energy will pull down the yang energy entering your home, so keep the powder room door closed. If the powder room is not opposite the front door, put a

mirror on the outside of the powder room door to make it symbolically disappear. If you have a bathroom off the master bedroom, always keep the door closed, as you do not want the waste energies from this area disrupting the calm, yin energies in the bedroom. In all bathrooms keep the toilet seat down, and shut it when flushing to preserve chi loss. Plants and candles will help to lift the sluggish energy here.

12

13 Study your yard thoroughly. In the front yard and by your driveway, make sure that there are no overgrown or unruly shrubs preventing visitors from entering your home. Look for any broken gates or fences that let your boundaries down, and get them repaired as soon as you can. Check the paths to the home, at both the front and the back. They should be winding, but if any path is straight, you can break it up by placing pots containing flowering plants at intervals along the path. If the back garden is full of weeds, deal with these as soon as possible as they are strangling you symbolically .

14 If you have a shed, think about what you are storing there. If this space is full of rusty old tools and decaying outdoor furniture, you are pulling down the energetics of the home, even if the shed is sited quite a way from the house. Throw out what is not needed and store all items neatly, putting smaller items on shelves or hanging them from hooks.

15

14

15 Look at your garage, if you have one. This is a storage space, but often contains so much trash that there is no room for the cars. If your garage is attached to the house, the stagnancy will filter into the home, so clear it out and plan good storage. If there is a bedroom over the garage, the stagnancy from the garage can filter upward so find the middle part of the ceiling and stick a large piece of natural quartz here to neutralize the bad energies.

FRONT DOOR AND ENTRY HALL

THIS AREA IS the "mouth" of the home where chi first enters, and it is the place where friends and family are welcomed. It is here that people get their first impression of the character of your home. The atmosphere here can feel pleasant and inviting or perhaps a little dull and dark if the area has been neglected for a while. How the entry hall looks and feels will influence whether your visitors want to return.

An entry hall needs to be bright and vibrant but also practical for everyday living, with adequate storage for paraphernalia such as umbrellas, outdoor clothes, shoes, and boots so that this area remains clutterfree and with a good, positive energy flow through to the rest of the home.

Light pastel shades on the walls can really open up the area, and mirrors can create the illusion of much more space (see pages 82–83), particularly when one is placed on a wall in a narrow entry hall. Good lighting from pendant fixtures, downlighters, or spotlights increases the presence of the yang energy that is needed here, making any entry feel more charming, inviting, and vibrant. Increase the appeal and liven up the atmosphere of your entry hall— and see how many exciting new people and opportunities enter your life.

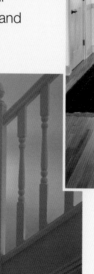

THE INNER SPACE

Entry halls vary in size and shape, of course, ranging from a large and impressive room to a tiny area with only enough space for a small table and a coat rack. Whatever the size of the entry hall, it is important to have a steady flow of positive chi, because it is from here that the chi winds its way through the rest of your home. This is where close friends and loved relatives are welcomed into your nest, your special living space. It should be painted in light, bright colors but have a coziness and warmth that draw in the people you want to see regularly in your home.

Sometimes energy can move too fast through an entry hall. A typical problem occurs when a staircase is opposite the front door; energy will rush up the stairs unless it is slowed down with a five-rod metal wind chime (see page 53). A similar problem occurs if the front and back doors are opposite each other—this can be corrected by placing two tall round-leaved plants at intervals down the hall to filter and slow the energy flow.

Good lighting is needed in the entry hall to brighten the space and welcome people in.

A mirror on one of the side walls in the entry hall enlarges the space and brings in yang energy.

A hall table can hold inviting plants or flowers and store keys and mail.

RIGHT Choose
inspirational art or
photos that you will love
looking at.

Paint the entry hall in a light pastel shade to
bring in more light.

Keep the entry hall clutterfree and tidy as this is
the "mouth and throat" of the home and where
energy first enters.

Clutter checklist

Clutter has no place in the entry hall, as the stagnancy it creates will stifle the energy just when it enters your home. Piles of clutter lying around will also leave a musty, unpleasant smell. Look out for the following junk and remove it:

- Take out work bags, briefcases, and computer bags that have been dumped here, and transfer them to the study.
- Remove children's strollers, bicycles, or skateboards, and store them in a cupboard or outdoors in the shed.
- Muddy boots, shoes, sneakers, and hiking boots are better put away in a shoe cupboard than piled up on the floor. Discard outgrown or worn-out footwear.
- Hang well-loved coats and jackets in the coat closet or on a coat rack or hooks. Discard tired, torn, or abandoned coats.
- Throw out old keys and hang current ones on hooks near the door.

Lively art

To personalize your entry hall, put up interesting and inspiring art or photographs that depict the flavor of your home life. You may want to show a happy family atmosphere with fun pictures of you, your partner, and your children on the walls. Or perhaps you are single, adore traveling, and want to line the walls with colorful, evocative shots of markets, temples, countryside, and street scenes from the wonderful places you have visited. Bring in your future by placing images on the walls of what you desire in your life: if you are longing to move to a new home, for example, add inspiring pictures of the type of architecture or the countries or localities in which you are interested. If you desire a new relationship, put up pictures of happy, loving couples.

WHAT NOT TO DO
If you have a staircase opposite your door, the energy that enters your home will travel too fast up it. To slow it down you will need to place a five-rod metal wind chime over the inside of the door.

LIGHT UP YOUR ENTRY HALL

Good lighting and the right mirror can boost the energy flow in your entry hall and really brighten up this space, which can sometimes be a bit dull and dark.

Mirrors will double the energy of the space in which they are placed. Position a mirror on a side wall in the entry hall, ideally reflecting a pleasant picture, a healthy plant, or lovely flowers. Mirrors come in a variety of shapes and sizes, so when choosing one try to match the shape to your door's element:

✦ For a Fire entrance, look for a star-shaped mirror or one that has a zig-zag pattern.

✦ Hang up an oval or round mirror for a Metal doorway.

✦ If it is an Earth door, use a square or rectangular mirror.

✦ For a Wood door choose a tall, vertical mirror.

✦ With a Water entrance you can have a bit of fun and use a free-flowing or wavy-shaped mirror.

Also match the lighting to its element where possible, but otherwise choose fittings to match the room's style. Be expansive—a small chandelier with lead-crystal drops, for example, can look wonderful in a wide traditional entry hall or one that has a dramatic entrance. Downlighters are perfect for illuminating a modern entry hall and give strong, even light. If you are on a budget, a track of spotlights can suit all styles of decoration and bring in plenty of yang energy, while single spotlights light up favorite pictures or well-loved photographs.

LEFT With a combination of a large side mirror and good pendant light or downlighters, you bring in the yang chi needed in the entry hall.

OVAL MIRROR FOR METAL ENTRY HALL
An ornate mirror will suit the foyer of a traditional home. The oval shape is associated with the Metal element, so will strengthen a west entry hall.

CHANDELIER TO BOOST THE ENERGY
A large entry hall can often benefit from a chandelier, as the reflection from the glass or crystal drops speeds up the flow of chi in this yang environment.

WAVY MIRROR FOR WATER ENTRY HALL
A modern home can suit the unconventional style of a wavy mirror. The shape emulates the flow of water and so will enhance an entry hall in the north.

RECTANGULAR MIRROR FOR EARTH ENTRY
Having lights either side of a mirror in an entry hall will double its yang energy. A rectangular mirror links to Earth, so site one in southwest and northeast entries.

UPLIGHTERS FOR A DARK ENTRY HALL
If you have a dark entry hall, paint it a light tone of its element color. Increase the level of yang chi by placing an uplighter next to a table or pictures.

THE LIVING ROOM

EVERYONE LOVES to relax in the living room—this is the part of your home where you can finally wind down after a long day's work. Here you can put your feet up and doze, or closet yourself with a good book, insulated from the busy world outside your front door. Calm vibrations should wrap themselves around you, making you feel cosseted and tranquil.

The living room is also the social hub of the home where everyone catches up on the day's news and where friends and relatives are entertained. Often the room is dual-purpose, with one section for relaxing and the other for casual meals and dinner parties or perhaps a small office. Demarcating these zones with plants, bookcases, or screens is important, as you need to fill the living space with yin energy while pumping up the dining or study area with yang chi for convivial meals or creative thinking.

Choose comfortable, supportive sofas (see pages 90–91) as you will spend a lot of your spare time being soothed and calmed by them. Display cherished possessions on shelving or in glass-fronted cabinets (see pages 94–95) so that you can admire them while you are seated. Clever combination units can house your television, your DVD player, and all your DVDs and CDs, keeping them off the floor and tidy.

Luxurious soft furnishings, treasured mementos, adored furniture, and well-chosen accessories will turn this room into the delightful haven you are seeking.

A VITAL HAVEN

The living room is where all the family relaxes at the end of a busy day. It is a social center where friends and relatives gather, so a steady flow of chi is essential here for convivial vibes. Make sure you keep it clutterfree, particularly in hidden corners to prevent any stagnancy.

Get happy!

Choose comfortable, well-padded, rounded sofas and chairs so that you can really relax in them. Plan your seating so that it is all grouped around a central coffee table or in front of a fire to encourage lively conversation. Arrange sofas carefully to optimize harmony (see pages 90–91) and don't be tempted to add too many chairs and side tables as you will cramp the flow of chi. A sense of security is important where you are sitting, so avoid placing your main seating under beams, which give off harmful cutting chi, or under a sloping ceiling, which will make you feel confined or restless.

Plants absorb pollutants and are good energizers in the living room.

Long, flowing curtains are yin. They soften a tall window and balance the yang elements such as the fireplace.

Cream shades on the walls make a living room seem larger and will bring in calming energy in a Fire element room.

A coffee table helps create symmetry in your seating arrangement and invites social gatherings.

A wooden floor allows chi to flow freely in the room.

Lift the atmosphere

Round-leafed plants and cut flowers are wonderful energizers in the living room. Place them around the room on windowsills and on coffee tables and side tables. Tall plants give out more oxygen; they can slow down fast chi flowing between two doors, and can also absorb any pollutants from the atmosphere or from synthetic furniture.

ABOVE Attractive flowers can be displayed on storage units. They also help to brighten up dark corners.

Lamps give background lighting and boost yang energy in the room.

Choose the art on your walls carefully. Avoid any depressing or turbulent pictures that may upset the home's harmony.

A fireplace is the focal point of a living room and draws people to it. Decorating the mantel with plants, lighting, *objets*, and pictures will add to its appeal.

High-backed, comfy sofas and big plump pillows give support and help you unwind.

Clutter checklist

Having loads of clutter scattered around the living room will affect the ambience and pull down the room's vitality. Check the following areas in particular, and remove any unwanted items:

✦ Look behind sofas and check for any forgotten packets of photographs, discarded electronic games, or abandoned craft or hobby projects.

✦ Search for old magazines, catalogs, and newspapers under coffee tables and in magazine racks, and bundle them up for recycling.

✦ Go through your DVD, video, and CD collections. Keep the ones you love but remove any that you no longer watch or listen to. Sell them to a secondhand shop or online retailer or give them to your local thrift shop or a rummage sale.

✦ Appraise all the *objets* you have in the room. If you have too many or you just don't like some any more, move them on by selling them or giving them away to a thrift shop.

✦ Be ruthless about your collection of books, as you need to allow space for new titles. Give unwanted paperbacks to a local library or hospital and put hardbacks aside for a rummage sale or garage sale.

WHAT NOT TO DO
Be careful how you position the seating in your living room. Placing sofas directly opposite each other can be confrontational, and you may find your guests having unprovoked arguments or disagreements.

Lighten up the room

Subtle tones of cream, yellow, or soft pastel colors will make a living space appear larger and create a deeply relaxed atmosphere. If you want to enjoy a really peaceful environment, paint the room in a shade of the color linked to the calming element of the room. For example, in a Fire room you would bring in shades of yellow or beige, because Earth calms Fire in the element cycle (see pages 20–21).

Plan lighting to improve the ambience of the room. Uplighters, downlighters, or wall sconces provide background lighting, while floor or table lamps can be strategically positioned for task lighting. Use spotlights for accent lighting on sculptures, plants, pictures, a display cabinet, or bookcases.

Scented candles give a glorious aroma and subtle glow when placed on a mantelpiece or a windowsill, adding a feeling of warmth in the winter and a romantic or cozy atmosphere at other times.

ABOVE Floor lamps add ambient lighting to a living room. This shape, similar to a star, supports the Fire element in a south living room.

LEFT If you have an open or fuel-effect fire, it is natural to position your sofas and chairs around it. This low coffee table harmonizes and balances the seating.

LEFT Wicker sofas with comfy cushions can add an Indian style to a living room. A matching table and lamp fill the room with natural fibers.

Lower your EMFs

All electrical equipment emits an electromagnetic field, which can make you feel lethargic and lacking in energy when you are regularly exposed to it. To help protect you and your family from this radiation, put plants in front of any stereo systems, televisions, and DVD players to absorb the emissions. Alternatively, you can place a piece of lepidolite or fluorite crystal next to the equipment, which will also reduce the impact of this negative energy.

RIGHT Scented candles add a lovely smell to the living room in the evening, while emitting a soft background glow.

BELOW Plants add yang energy to a living room. They can also soak up any electromagnetic emissions from electrical equipment.

Balance your yin and yang

To get the right balance of energetic harmony in this social space, you need to blend the yin (soft) and yang (hard) accessories. For example, if you have a yang hardwood dining table, balance it with full, flowing curtains or with wool or cotton throws. Mirrors and glass furniture or shelving (all yang) can be countered with rugs, tapestry screens, or wicker or rattan furniture (all yin).

SOFAS

Comfortable seating is one of your prime concerns in the living room for real relaxation. So choose sofas in a variety of tactile or more practical fabrics. In feng shui terms a sofa with a high back, large comfy cushions, and rounded arms is the best type to buy as it will give support and you will avoid any negative chi that comes off square corners. This is especially important for the stylish L-shaped sofas. Some sofas have removable headrests, which helps to give additional support when you are sitting for a long time. Removable, washable slipcovers are a good option to keep sofas looking fresh and chi levels high.

Choose sofas to match either the element of the room or its calming element to achieve maximum relaxation. For example, if you have a Fire room, buy a yellow or beige sofa as Earth calms Fire in the Exhaustive cycle. Alternatively, if you have a Wood room, opt for red sofas as Fire calms Wood in the Exhaustive cycle.

Plan your sofa layout well. Try to group them at angles to each other rather than positioned opposite, which can be too confrontational. Also, avoid placing a sofa directly facing a door, as you will feel drained by the force of incoming chi. Ideally, position any sofa next to a wall for security. However, if you do have to place it away from the wall, create some support behind it using a storage unit or a low bookcase.

BELOW Modern sofas with side returns make a sociable and convivial shape for entertaining your friends and family.

ROUNDED ARMS FOR GOOD CHI
Padded, rounded arms on sofas are comfortable for resting against, and the smooth scroll shape means no sha chi is directed from the sofa into the room.

RED SOFA FOR FIRE ROOM
A red sofa is ideal in a south living room (Fire). However, be careful of having too much white with it, as Metal controls Fire in the Destructive element cycle.

WICKER SOFAS FOR SUNROOMS
Wicker sofas give a colonial feel to light-filled sunrooms. Their natural fibers will enhance the atmosphere and insure a good circulation of chi.

FLOWING SHAPES AND CONVERSATION
Matching sofas grouped around a coffee table in a semicircle help conversation to flow freely and easily between all your guests.

WHITE SOFAS LINK TO METAL
A white leather sofa can look stunning in a modern living area. It is best in a Metal living room or it can help to calm an Earth room.

CHIC LITTLE TABLES

It's essential in a living room to include occasional tables such as side tables and coffee tables to hold drinks and nibbles, books and magazines, and to display energizing plants or flowers. In addition, side tables make ideal sites for table lamps, while coffee tables can help to bring seating arrangements together. Grouping chairs and sofas around a small table encourages good chi flow around the room and creates a harmonious arrangement.

In general, round and oval tables are the best to have in your living room as they allow chi to move positively and have no sharp edges that can give off bad or cutting energy.

Try to link the occasional tables you choose to the element of the living room, in order to strengthen the energy already existing there. For example, if you have an Earth room, a square table will enhance it, whereas if it is a Metal room, a round or oval-shaped table will support it.

You can also bring yin and yang into your table selection. Wicker side tables are very yin and can be used in a living room to balance yang items such as mirrors, glass furniture, or stone floors. On the other hand, a small yang hardwood table can balance a living room's yin furnishings such as carpets, rugs, or flowing curtains.

BELOW A roughly hewn coffee table can be used to effect in a country home. Friends will naturally be drawn around it to enjoy the warmth of the fire.

GLASS TABLES ARE WATER ELEMENT
A round table promotes prosperity, and when it is glass, or Water element, it is best placed in a Water room to support the energies of a room in the north.

FLUID SHAPES HELP CHI FLOW
Stacking side tables with rounded, flowing edges help to create a balanced atmosphere as they let chi energy move smoothly around them.

ROUNDED SHAPES FOR GOOD CHI
Plexiglas side tables with simple, curved lines will help prevent negative, cutting chi from being aimed at people sitting within the living room.

ENERGIZING PLANTS AND FLOWERS
Side tables can be decorated with vibrant plants or flowers that will add vitality to your living room. Keep your accessories simple to avoid clutter.

SQUARE TABLES SUPPORT EARTH
A square side table links to the nurturing element of Earth, so it is good for displaying light offerings, such as bowls of snacks, when friends visit.

OVAL TABLES ARE METAL ELEMENT
An oval shape represents the Metal element, so an oval table will help to lift the energies in a living room located in the west of your home.

STORAGE UNITS TO CLEAR CLUTTER

Classy storage units really bring together the design of a living room and will help to keep possessions off the floor and neatly housed, which will aid chi flow. If you are a book lover, it can be a good idea to have bookcases built in to your own requirements. However, freestanding pieces work just as well and they can be attached to the wall to prevent any accidents. If the shelving has hard edges, bring the books forward so that they are flush with the fronts of the shelves, softening the line and preventing any poison arrows from being directed at you.

A television unit can house the television, DVD player, VCR, and any other cable-receiving devices. Many units let you feed the cabling through the back, keeping this area tidy and clutterfree. DVDs and CDs can be stored in integral or separate units. Many ingenious designs are produced for them now.

Tall glass and wood cabinets to display treasured collections or china and glass can fit neatly into corners or be a feature of the room. Try to buy furniture with rounded corners as much as possible to avoid harmful cutting chi.

BELOW If you love displaying artifacts or if you have an extensive book collection, it is a good idea to have some storage units built to your requirements.

TELEVISION UNIT FOR NEAT STORAGE
As well as holding the television, a storage unit like this can store the VCR or DVD-player and conceal disks, remote controls, and instruction manuals.

MULTIFUNCTIONAL UNIT
Units that include a mirror can help to expand the space in a small room. Store items that you love and use regularly, and don't hang on to junk.

USEFUL STORAGE BOXES
Natural seagrass boxes in different sizes can look attractive in a corner of the living room. Store magazines, brochures, candles, or spare table linen in them.

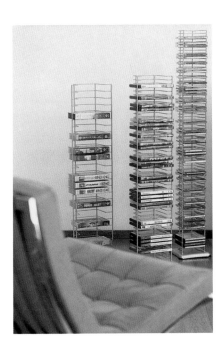

GOOD CD STORAGE
If you are a music lover, you will need adequate storage for your CD collection. These metal towers store many disks and look stylish.

ROUNDED STORAGE FOR GOOD CHI
Simple, rounded storage units help chi flow. They can store a few books that you are currently reading and hold a cup of coffee as well as a lamp.

INTERESTING ORIENTAL STORAGE
Hardwood storage units from Asia bring a yang element into the living room and create an Eastern style that can be emphasized with statues of dancers or musicians.

AUSPICIOUS WINDOW TREATMENTS

Curtains in coordinating fabrics can bring together the decorating scheme in your living room. If you have a dark room, long, flowing silk or muslin curtains will allow some light to penetrate. All curtains slow down the flow of chi, which is fine in the living room as the emphasis here is on calm. Heavier fabrics such as velvets and damasks slow chi further and can suit a large traditional living room or help to shut out the noise and disturbance from a busy street.

To emphasize the room's element, remember to choose curtains with the appropriate color and pattern. If you have a Fire room, put up red curtains with a triangular, star, or zigzag pattern. In an Earth room use yellow or beige and square or rectangular designs. For a Wood room, a subtle vertical striped pattern on green fabric is best. For a Metal room choose circular or oval patterns on white fabrics. For a Water room, go for wavy or irregular patterns on blue or black material.

Blinds and shades can also feature their element pattern. The soft horizontal folds of Roman shades work well in a Water room as they emulate the gently flowing movement of the element. In a very sunny Wood room, wooden Venetian blinds are ideal for shielding furniture from the bleaching effects of sunlight.

RIGHT Heavier flowing draperies suit tall windows in traditional rooms. They slow down chi flow, keep out cold drafts, and help reduce traffic noise.

PLEATED CURTAINS FOR STRUCTURE
This neat style of pleated curtains adds elegant definition to a living room. The curtains seem to give the room some structure and order.

STRIPED CURTAINS LINK TO WOOD
If you need to emphasize the Wood element in your living room, feature some striped curtains, as stripes are associated with this element.

FINE FABRICS LIGHTEN ROOMS
Fine muslin curtains will let more light into a dark living room and illuminate brighter spaces. Painting the room in a light shade of its element also increases light.

NATURAL BLINDS FOR HARMONY
Wicker or bamboo matchstick blinds can be an inexpensive solution for the living room. As they are natural materials, they smooth chi movement in the room.

ROMAN SHADES LINK TO WATER ELEMENT
The soft folds of Roman shades emulate the gentle movement of the Water element, so can be ideal to support this element in a north living room.

VENETIAN BLINDS FOR SUN PROTECTION
Venetian blinds allow light into the living room but, when open, also give some protection from strong, yang sunlight, which can bleach furniture.

THE DINING ROOM

THE DINING ROOM is the place where you entertain your friends and family and enjoy good food and conversation. Having family meals here daily will allow everyone to share their news and promote good communication among family members. Even if you live alone or do not have a separate dining area, make the space where you eat a special, harmonious place.

Not much furniture is needed here—a table, comfortable chairs, and a sideboard, hutch, or china cabinet will suffice. As the table is the main piece of furniture, choose the style you want carefully. Round tables are the most auspicious to use in the dining room, but square or rectangular ones are also beneficial (see pages 104–105). Have comfortable, supportive chairs—six or eight is an auspicious number—as you may well be lingering over long, leisurely meals.

Keep the yang energies high here with color, good lighting, flowers and plants. Paint the room in its element color or use the energizing element (see page 21). Good lighting (see page 101) makes people feel joyful, while soft candlelight creates a romantic environment for those special occasions or anniversaries. Adorn the sideboard and table with fresh flowers and fruit to bring abundance into all areas of your life.

DINING BLISS

With today's busy lifestyles in which everyone is dashing off in different directions, the dining room can be one of the rooms in the home where everybody gathers for a filling evening meal or a leisurely Sunday lunch. This is the place of fun, laughter, lively conversation, and good food. Families are reunited and friendships are revived in this space during the eating of delicious and nutritious food.

It is important to spend some time destressing while sitting down and feeding your body and mind rather than rushing around and eating meals on the go. It doesn't matter if you have a large, spacious dining room or a tiny area in your living room; make it your own sacred space for lingering over appetizing, nourishing meals.

Happy seating

The table is the main piece of furniture in the dining room, so choose the style you want carefully (see pages 104–105). If you have a through living/dining room, it is a good idea to demarcate the two areas with a screen or a bookcase. But whether your dining area is part of an open-plan living area or a separate dining room, as a convivial and social space it should not be cramped and dark or overcrowded with furniture.

Placing the table centrally opposite a window allows plenty of light for lunchtime eating.

A good light is essential over the dining table to increase the yang energy for eating.

A rectangular hardwood table is beneficial and very yang.

Make sure the table is placed centrally for good ventilation and the minimum of drafts. Avoid siting it near doorways so that the fast incoming chi does not make people restless when they are seated at the table having a leisurely lunch or dinner. If there are two doors into your dining room, keep them closed when eating so that you are not affected by fast chi flow.

The right ambience

Pendant lighting over a dining table or light from downlighters can highlight the food you are eating and make it seem even more appetizing.

Candles are a gentle energizer, wonderful for an intimate dinner party or sensuous meal for two. Red or pink candles will add love and romance, but if you want more passion bring in red place settings, tablecloths, and napkins.

Mirrors are excellent energy-expanders; place one opposite the table to double the food on the table, symbolizing wealth and abundance for the household. Fresh flowers are great energizers, too. You can also increase the yang energies of this area, making it a more vibrant spot to eat, by placing healthy round-leaved plants around the room.

A cabinet positioned near the table will insure that glasses are handy for meals.

BELOW Padded chairs with supportive backs will facilitate leisurely eating.

ABOVE Oval tables are good in the dining room because they give off no cutting chi. A glass table will support a Water room.

Clutter checklist

Clutter is not usually such an issue in the dining room but watch out for the following items that may be scattered around, lowering the room's positive energy:

✦ Check in sideboard drawers for old, unused silverware, torn napkins and discolored placemats and junk.

✦ Look through your glasses cabinet and throw away any that are chipped or cracked as they lower energy. Give unused or disliked sets to a thrift shop.

✖ WHAT NOT TO DO

Do not clutter up a dining room—just have a table, chairs, and a cabinet or sideboard. Placing the table opposite an open fire would make it too hot for pleasurable dining.

CREATIVE TABLE SETTINGS

Table settings really bring a dining room scheme together. Elegant wine glasses, eye-catching candlesticks, stylish tableware, and coordinating placemats and tablecloths make every meal special. Avoid man-made tablecloths and napkins and buy table linen in natural fabrics, which let chi flow freely and smoothly. If the surface of your table is not particularly attractive, a tablecloth will effectively disguise the fact. If you prefer an Eastern theme, use silk runners in colourful Japanese or Indian designs with

matching placemats, or rush mats and oriental-style candles to complete the look. Bold, modern, practical tableware that is dishwasher- and microwave-safe will work for all types of households, whether you are a family or a single person living on your own.

Match patterns to your room's element or its energizing element to bring further harmony (see pages 20–31). For a Metal room, for example, choose designs with big circular patterns on a white background to match the element; or if

you want to energize a Metal dining room, select a square or rectangular design on a yellow or beige background (Earth feeds Metal in the element cycle). If you like simple white tableware but have a room that needs Fire energy, you could introduce some red or pink placemats, napkins, and candles. Silver or iron candlesticks are perfect to enhance a Metal room, while china ones will support an Earth room. Interesting carved wooden candlesticks will strengthen a Wood room or can energize a Fire room.

LEFT Light green plates will emphasize the energy in a Wood room. Adding a fresh flower as natural decoration looks beautiful and will also bring in more Wood energy.

WHITE PLATES FOR ELEGANCE
Elegant white table settings can look stunning on a white tablecloth or a plain wooden table. Yellow flowers bring in some boosting yang energy.

MODERN METAL STYLE
Stylish metal table accessories set off the simplicity of white tableware. They both link to the Metal element, so are ideal in northwest and west rooms.

ORIENTAL PLACE SETTINGS
If you are serving a Thai or Chinese meal for guests, using bowls and chopsticks plus a natural centerpiece, such as wheatgrass, really sets the scene.

INTIMATE CANDLE GLOW
Adding some candles to your table setting lends a warmth and intimate glow and a bit of yang energy that is just right for an evening dinner party with friends.

COUNTRY TABLE STYLE
If you have a rustic style of table, adding accessories such as a single candlestick and a pitcher of garden flowers can bring a natural grace to a dinner party.

TABLE RUNNERS FOR DECORATION
An oriental-style runner or one with a delicate pattern can liven up a table for a dinner party or add a bit of interest when the table is not in use.

HARMONIOUS TABLE SHAPES

Enjoying a well-cooked meal in pleasant surroundings and with fun guests is one of the pleasures of life. Finding the right dining table for eating convivial meals is very important in feng shui. The table's shape is particularly crucial:

✦ A round table is very yang and is the best style to use because it has no sharp corners and so allows chi to move smoothly. The round shape also represents heaven luck and is linked to money.

✦ An oval table also has no corners and allows chi to move freely, so it, too, is auspicious. However, it has more yin energies and therefore is better suited to casual dining.

✦ Square and rectangular styles of table are both auspicious, but a square shape is always best for yang dining and dinner parties, while a rectangular table induces more relaxed eating. Avoid sitting any guests at the sharp corners of these tables because they

could end up suffering from indigestion or stomach pains.

Buy comfortable, supportive chairs for dining. High-backed upholstered chairs are ideal as your guests will feel secure and comfortable sitting on them for hours. Very modern metallic styles with metal struts and criss-cross seating are not favorable in feng shui as they can give off cutting chi. Wooden chairs with padded backs and seats will also encourage long, relaxed dining.

LEFT An oval table has no harsh corners and this one can seat six or eight people. The shape is well suited to casual lunches and suppers.

SQUARE YANG TABLE
A square table is the best shape for lively dinner parties and lunches, as it is a very yang shape. You can soften its sharp corners with a tablecloth.

ROUND TABLE FOR PROSPERITY
A round table is the perfect shape in feng shui as chi moves smoothly around it and it is associated with money. A chandelier brings in more yang energy.

PADDED CHAIRS FOR HAPPY EATING
Choose chairs with padded seats and supportive backs to make sure that your guests are comfortable and at ease when enjoying your meals.

MODERN TABLE STYLE
High-backed modern chairs lend style to your dining table. If the seats become uncomfortable during long dinners, add some seat pads.

GLASS TABLE FOR WATER ROOM
A glass table is ideal in a Water room, as it links to this element. The white metal chairs give some feeding energy, which is perfect for dining purposes.

THE KITCHEN

NOWADAYS THE KITCHEN is usually the hub of the home, where all the family gather to chat and catch up on the news of the day as the evening meal is being prepared. In feng shui terms it is the "heart" of the home and should be a warm, light, cozy, and nurturing environment that everybody loves. As this space is all about nourishment and health, you need to keep the yang energies high here for everybody's continuing well-being. Keep the atmosphere bright and welcoming, especially if this is a space where you eat regularly or where friends sit when they have come around for a coffee and a chat.

Fire and Water are the major elements in the kitchen but because they are incompatible, it is important to take care with the positioning of your fridge, freezer, cooktop, oven, and sink. To keep a strong chi flow that inspires you when you are cooking and serving meals, avoid cluttering the countertops with appliances. Planning in enough storage units will help to keep the work surfaces clear (see pages 110–111).

Balance the strong yang presence of the kitchen with some yin accessories such as curtains or shades, dish towels, and wicker baskets.

THE SOCIAL HUB

The kitchen is where everybody seems to congregate, whether it is dinner guests gathering to talk to the cook preparing a meal, children rushing in after school to share the events of the day or friends dropping in for an intimate chat after an argument. Maybe the warmth and the delicious cooking smells are what draw everybody to the kitchen, or simply the fact that the food prepared and often eaten here nourishes everyone and keeps them healthy and vital. Support the yang energy needed in the kitchen with strong lighting, uncluttered surfaces, and well-planned storage.

Boost the chi

In the past, siting the kitchen in the south, southeast or east of the home was often preferred as it linked in with the Productive cycle of the five elements, but nowadays keeping chi beneficial is seen as more important here. This is easiest to do when you are planning a new kitchen, but there are also ways of improving the chi in existing kitchens.

If you are fitting out a new kitchen, allow for plenty of storage units so that you will be able to keep appliances and food off the countertops. Use a round-leaved plant to deflect and soften any cutting chi coming off a sharp corner unit that is close to the sink or cooking area.

The cooktop and oven are the kitchen's heart, so ideally they should be sited away from the freezer, refrigerator, and sink, as the elements Fire and Water are in conflict. If you have no option, or have inherited a bad arrangement, put a metal item between them to control this volatile energy.

Strong lighting will boost the yang energy needed in the kitchen.

Keep the fridge-freezer full of healthy food to demonstrate the prosperity of the home.

The cooktop and oven are the kitchen's heart, so use all the burners regularly and keep them spotless.

A movable butcher block can be useful for extra work space in the kitchen.

ABOVE Keeping the kitchen clean and tidy will insure that vitality is high here. Empty all garbage cans on a regular basis to reduce stagnancy.

Try to make sure that the cooktop and oven do not face the front door. If they do, keep the door closed or use some form of screening, such as a beaded curtain. Houseplants will lift the energy, feeding more oxygen into the environment, and can also slow energy flow if two doors are opposite each other.

Good ventilation is important in the kitchen, so position it away from a powder room or bathroom. If there is no choice, keep the doors between them closed so that the bathroom or toilet waste energies and odors do not penetrate the food preparation area.

Good ceiling lighting, as well as lighting under the upper cabinets, will increase yang chi and make the space bright and appealing for cooking.

If there is a table or breakfast bar in the kitchen, one or more pendant lights fitted above them will provide effective task lighting. Spotlights or downlighters would also work well here.

Hygiene and cleanliness are essential in the kitchen, so avoid a buildup of trash, laundry, or dirty dishes. Train everyone in your family to load the dishwasher straightaway and to wash anything that cannot be put in it.

Clutter checklist

Clutter needs to be addressed in this room quickly or you will pull down its inspiring energy. Check out the following items that could lower the energetics:

✦ Search through cabinets and get rid of out-of-date sauces, oils, vinegars, packaged goods, or cans, which reduce energy levels.

✦ If you have a growing mountain of bottles, newspapers, and cartons, recycle them and reuse any plastic or paper bags.

✦ Empty garbage cans daily, as they breed stagnancy.

✦ Go through your refrigerator and freezer regularly and remove any food that has been lingering there too long.

Yellow is a good boosting color to use in a Metal kitchen, or it can enhance an Earth kitchen.

Keep only essential utensils on the countertops so that chi can flow freely.

The sink should always be positioned well away from the fridge-freezer and the cooktop and oven.

Include plenty of cabinets to hold all your kitchen products and appliances.

WHAT NOT TO DO
Cluttering up a kitchen will disrupt the movement of chi, making it sluggish and lethargic, and will lower the yang energy needed in this busy area. Store small appliances out of sight in cabinets.

EFFECTIVE STORAGE

A well-planned kitchen with cabinets and countertops filling the available space will be pleasing to the eye as well as a pleasure to use. Take time planning the design of your kitchen cabinets as you always need more than you think. Most manufacturers will do a plan to your design and will normally be inventive with the area you have available.

Storing your kitchen goods in cabinets will keep chi flowing well. Many lower cabinets with deep drawers now have partitioned inserts for neatly storing wine glasses, saucepans, plates, and silverware. Tall pantry units can hold all your store cupboard provisions.

Match your cabinets to their energizing element color:

✦ For a Wood room use blue or black cabinets as Water feeds Wood.

✦ For a Fire room plan in Wood or green cabinets as Wood feeds Fire.

✦ For an Earth room add red cabinets as Fire feeds Earth.

✦ For a Metal room choose yellow or beige cabinets as Earth feeds Metal.

✦ For a Water room use white or metallic cabinets as Metal feeds Water.

For a freer, less built-in look, a movable butcher block with shelves underneath or a metal wheeled cart is useful. Not only will it aid food preparation but it will also provide storage for items such as kitchen linen, wine bottles, or bottles of water.

BELOW Hanging rails fitted on the wall behind a countertop can create that extra storage needed for kitchen utensils that you use on a regular basis.

TALL CABINET FOR PRODUCTS
If you have a family, consider installing a tall pull-out pantry storage unit to hold all your kitchen produce. They can often be made to fit into small, redundant spaces, too.

CLEVER PULL-OUT CORNER CABINETS
In tight corners, fit cabinets that pull out to one side so everything is easier to reach. Dried goods can be stored in separate compartments for fast access.

USEFUL ROUNDED UNITS
Rounded units aid the flow of chi and can be built around the curves of countertops. They can hold bottles, canned goods, and other products.

INGENIOUS DRAWER UNITS
Spices, knives, and other kitchen necessities can be stored right out of sight in these clever drawer units which have been designed with special inserts.

NEAT STORAGE FOR POTS
Big casseroles and other oven dishes can be stored in spacious, pull-out lower cabinets so that they are all visible and close at hand when you are cooking.

MOVABLE KITCHEN STORAGE
A stylish wheeled kitchen cart is ideal where work surfaces are lacking in the smaller kitchen. It can be stored out of sight when it is not in use.

COUNTERTOP SPACE-SAVERS

Filling your kitchen with useful accessories can make your life easier, particularly if you have a busy lifestyle with little time for preparation and cooking. If you are a gadget person who loves using different whisks, spoons, and spatulas, fit a hanging rail behind the cooktop or under upper cabinets so they do not clutter up the counter and are accessible. It's surprising how many items can be hung up this way.

In a tiny kitchen put up shelving in wasted spaces. A narrow shelving unit or very shallow shelves take up almost no space but provide a valuable amount of storage for small items. Fill the shelves with storage jars for legumes, rice, pasta, and other store-cupboard staples. Wicker baskets can sit here storing fruit and vegetables, foil, rolls of paper towels, and other materials. These baskets also bring in some yin energy to balance the yang kitchen. The garbage can may be concealed inside the door of a lower cabinet. You can also fit an ingenious unit that stores a pull-out ironing board in a small drawer.

If you don't have enough room for your silverware, fit Plexiglas flatware stands to the wall above the countertop. Simple accessories such as hidden hooks or rails to hang dish towels, or a napkin holder, plate rack, or paper-towel holder will help to keep your kitchen looking tidy and full of positive chi.

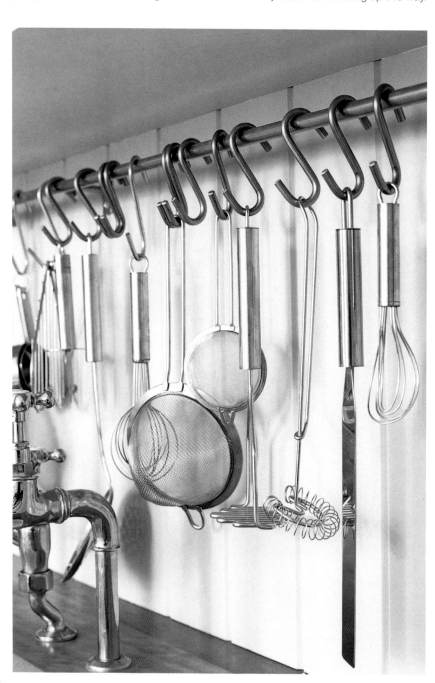

LEFT S-shaped hooks can be used with a hanging rail to enable you to store kitchen utensils that you often use in your day-to-day cooking.

PLATE RACK STORAGE
Special fittings can be inserted into solid drawers to store all your sets of plates and bowls snugly so that they do not slide around and are easily accessible.

HANGING SILVERWARE BASKET
If all your kitchen drawers are full, consider hanging a silverware basket from hooks above the work surface to hold all the pieces that you use daily.

WICKER BASKETS FOR GOOD CHI
Simple wicker baskets promote good chi flow and are ideal to hold fresh produce as well as sauces and oils. Store them on countertops or on shelves.

COUNTERTOP BASKETS
In a small kitchen in which you have limited drawer space, a wicker drawer unit on the countertop can be used to house dish towels, napkins, and silverware.

SHELVING IN UNUSED SPACES
If you are having trouble fitting all your kitchen storage pots into cupboards, put up some shelves in an unused space to keep them within easy reach.

PRACTICAL FLOORING

Flooring in a kitchen needs to be practical as well as stylish, because there is so much movement through this busy room. Many different types of flooring are available, but think what you want to achieve in the room. If you have wood cabinets, for example, a wooden floor would blend in but is quite yin, so if you wanted more energy in a lively kitchen, a stone or tiled floor would bring in more yang energy. However, if you have several boisterous children, this type of flooring will not prove very user-friendly, as mugs, bowls, or plates will break so easily on it. In this case, a good option is to fit laminate, vinyl, or linoleum, which are easy to clean and relatively forgiving if items are dropped on it.

Varnished wooden flooring is the boosting element for a Fire kitchen. It is warm and comfortable underfoot, and because of its neutral chi flow it will complement the yang presence of marble or granite countertops.

To keep yang energies high in the kitchen, match the color of the flooring to that of the boosting element (see pages 20–21). For example, if you have neutral beige kitchen units in an Earth kitchen, choose deep red sheet flooring or quarry tiles for more vitality, as Fire feeds Earth in the Productive cycle of elements.

LEFT A brick floor is associated with Earth and so it can give some of the uplifting energy needed in a Metal kitchen with white cabinets.

PRACTICAL KITCHEN FLOORING
Linoleum floor tiles can be a practical option in a busy kitchen as they are relatively inexpensive and are quick and easy to clean. The black and white tiles in particular look crisp and stylish.

CUSHIONED SHEET FLOORING
This flooring is a very durable choice for a kitchen floor and it is easy to clean. Because it is cushioned, ceramic items are less likely to break if dropped.

GROUNDING FLOOR TILES
Ceramic floor tiles are very hard-wearing and can feel grounding and earthy in the kitchen. They are very yang and can be contrasted with yin baskets and shades.

WOODEN FLOOR FOR NEUTRAL CHI
Varnished wooden flooring is great if you enjoy walking barefoot in the kitchen. It works well with gray cabinets as Water (blue/black) feeds Wood in the element cycle.

RUSTIC SLATE FLOOR
Slate flooring with its uneven surface and variations in color can look stunning in a country-style Earth kitchen. Cream cabinets also emphasize the Earth element.

THE BATHROOM

HAVING A REVIVING SHOWER or soaking in a scented bath in a luxurious bathroom after a hard day's work is one of the pleasures of life. Modern bathrooms are sanctuaries where you can indulge in some serious pampering. For the best atmosphere it's important to have a balance of yin and yang elements, and this is a challenge in a bathroom because the tiles, toilet, bath, shower stall, and sink (see pages 120–121) are all so yang. However, soft textiles and yin furniture and accessories can balance these elements.

Water is constantly draining in a bathroom, making it a very yin environment prone to stagnation. Steam from hot showers and baths also makes it very humid, slowing the flow of chi further. It will struggle even more in internal bathrooms that have no windows, making a good extractor fan a necessity.

Larger bathrooms will allow better chi flow but if you have a tiny bathroom, you can still lift the energy by careful planning of the bathroom suite and by clever use of color and textures. Candles, essential oils, and aromatic bath products (see pages 124–125) will fire up the energy, making the bathroom a sensual refuge from the rest of the world.

A SPA FOR THE SOUL

The bathroom is the place where you can close the door on your problems. It is here that you can hide from all the trials and tribulations of family life and just be yourself. You can lock the door, fill a bath with scented oil, and spend a languorous hour soaking away muscle aches, letting the problems of the day disappear, and allowing your spirit to soar once again. Here you cleanse body and soul, meditate on life, and consider new plans for the future. Your bathroom should be a place where you enjoy lingering for long periods of time.

Sites and layouts

The current trend is to have several bathrooms in a house or apartment, but think carefully about this as too many can become a drain on your finances.

A mirror placed over the sinks is essential for cleansing or shaving and will expand the space.

Having two sinks is a sensible option in a large bathroom so that two people can wash at the same time.

A reasonable-size shower stall allows space for perfect cleansing and can also take two people.

LEFT A traditional style of bathtub can be emphasized by a period mirror. A plant helps to speed up the sluggish energy flow in here.

A towel warmer will keep towels fresh and prevent any stagnancy in the bathroom.

This is particularly the case if one is positioned in the southeast, your Wealth area. When adding a new powder room to your home, do not site it opposite or alongside the front door as it can cause a conflict of yin and yang energies. If that position is unavoidable, always keep the powder room door closed. When adding a new bathroom, don't position it in the middle of your home as that would allow waste energies and odors to circulate everywhere.

Avoid having the toilet or bath opposite the door, as these are places where you need some privacy and protection. If you have inherited this bathroom layout, place a screen or some plants between the toilet or bath and the door. Make small bathrooms, especially ones with no windows, seem bigger by fitting a mirror on the wall over the sink as its energy will expand the space.

Light up the atmosphere

Strong lighting from downlighters will increase yang chi and boost the energy in the humid atmosphere of the bathroom. Color too can affect the room's ambience. Soft pinks and peaches are very soothing tones to live with, while a pale green is said to aid digestion. Blue links to flowing rivers, oceans, and lakes and can strengthen the flow of water in the room.

Place a good selection of healthy round-leafed house plants in the bathroom to bring in more chi.

Choose an enamel bathtub rather than a plastic one for long, luxurious bathing.

The toilet is best sited away from the door.

Ceramic floor tiles are practical in the bathroom as they are durable and easy to clean, but choose tiles with a nonslip finish, as they can be slippery when wet.

A good selection of healthy round-leaved houseplants will bring more chi into the room. If your bathroom is very humid or has lingering negativity, burn some candles or put some essential oils in the bath or an oil burner.

Clutter checklist

Having too much clutter will slow down the sluggish energy in the bathroom even more, so look out for the following items that may be lowering the chi here:

✦ Go through your medicine cabinets and throw out (or return to your pharmacist) any tablets, creams, or cough medicines that are past their expiry date or you will encourage more ill health in the family.

✦ Keep bath products off the bath or windowsill, throw away congealed or old ones and store the rest in a corner or a freestanding unit, to promote better chi flow.

✦ Take spare toilet paper and bath cleaning products off the floor and from around the bath, where they hinder chi flow, and store them in a vanity unit or other form of storage.

WHAT NOT TO DO
This sink is situated too near the doorway and may make you feel threatened while washing. Generally the bathroom is too cluttered. Have only a couple of storage units for good energy flow.

SINKS FOR FREE-FLOWING CHI

Sinks come in all shapes and sizes but whether they are ceramic or glass their hard surfaces speed up the flow of chi in the bathroom. Freestanding sinks are available in a variety of styles, ranging from a tiny hand-wash sink to a wide, old-fashioned Belle Epoque style. Or you could choose a sink that is inset into a vanity unit, which is particularly useful in a small bathroom where you have limited storage space.

✦ Round sinks have no harsh corners that could cause cutting chi in the bathroom. Because they link to the Metal element, they are particularly good in a west bathroom.

✦ Because glass resembles ice, glass sinks tend to be associated with the Water element.

✦ If you have an Earth bathroom, your best choice of sink is a square ceramic style, but try to make sure that any bad chi that can come off the corners does not hit the bath. If it does, place two plants in the line of the harsh chi to deflect it.

✦ A rectangular ceramic sink is the best type for a Wood room but again be careful with its placement.

BELOW A Belle Epoque sink will work well in a big bathroom. Its substantial top provides plenty of space to store essentials such as soap, toothpaste, and cleansers.

METAL SINK FOR WEST AND NORTHWEST
A metal sink like this stylish modern design supports Metal energy in northwest and west bathrooms. The glass surround brings in some calming energy.

CURVY SINK FOR WATER BATHROOM
This curvy style of sink is ideal for a bathroom in the north as its shape emulates the flow of water that is associated with the Water element.

SINK FOR A WEST ROOM
A round sink emphasizes the shape of the Metal element and so is the best shape to have in a bathroom where the energy comes in from the west.

ROUND SINK FOR POSITIVE CHI
A round sink insures a good movement of chi in the bathroom as there are no sharp corners to slow it down. Glass sinks also link to the Water element.

RECTANGULAR SINK FOR WOOD
Large rectangular sinks are associated with the Wood element, so will strengthen a southeast and east bathroom. The width allows plenty of space for washing.

CONICAL SINK FOR FIRE
The plant-pot shape of this sink links to the shape of the Fire element and so works best in a south bathroom. As it is so deep, the sink can hold a lot of water.

SHOWERS TO CLEANSE YOUR LIFE

Showers are a popular choice for modern living. A quick shower uses less water than a bath and is ideal in the morning when the whole family is in a rush to get ready for their busy day ahead. Tall showers with large, overhanging showerheads will help strengthen the chi in an east or northeast bathroom. Metal and white shower fixtures will particularly enhance the energy of a west bathroom.

Separate glass shower stalls are popular in large bathrooms and will support the Water energy of the north. They can give you a feeling of space and protection when showering, and are often big enough for two people to use at once.

If you have a shower fixture over a bath, a glass half door or screen will deflect water spillage and again give you some symbolic support. Shower curtains are a cheaper option and can be chosen, where possible, with attractive patterns to suit the room's element:

- ✦ White or metallic curtains with a circular pattern will give a boost to Metal bathrooms.
- ✦ Blue or black curtains with a wavy pattern are ideal for Water bathrooms.
- ✦ Pink or red curtains with a zigzag or star pattern will lift a Fire bathroom.
- ✦ Green curtains with a rectangular pattern accentuate the chi in a Wood bathroom.
- ✦ Yellow or beige curtains with square patterns will add more energy to an Earth bathroom.

LEFT Showering in a separate shower stall can make you feel safe and secure. You can also allow for a large showerhead to get a good spray of water.

ROUNDED SHOWER STALL
A rounded shower stall can fit neatly into a corner of the bathroom to maximize the use of space. The curved shape allows chi to flow around it easily.

HALF GLASS DOORS FOR BATH
When you have no room for a separate stall, a solution is to fit a shower over the bath and install glass doors for protection from the water spray.

DUAL SHOWERHEADS IN THE BATHROOM
Having two showerheads, one permanent and one handheld, allows you to take one off the wall to wash your hair. One showerhead may have different spray options.

LARGE SHOWERHEAD FOR A GOOD SPRAY
A large "watering can" style of showerhead works particularly well in a traditional bathroom. The large diameter allows for a generous spray of water.

SHOWER CURTAIN FOR A BATH
If you have a limited budget in the bathroom, a shower curtain can be a good option. Wash it regularly or replace it to avoid mold growth, which lowers the energetics.

CURVED SHOWER RAIL
A curved shower rail will follow the movement of chi and can be easily fitted around a bath. This blue shower curtain will support a Water bathroom.

MOOD ENHANCERS

Stylish, attractive bathrooms are now the norm in today's homes, even though they are considered negatively in feng shui terms as they drain so much water. Adding accent features to the bathroom will introduce natural elements, warmth, earthy textures, and lovely fragrances.

A seaside theme accentuates the Water element that is so strong here. Happy seaside pictures, pieces of driftwood, bowls of pebbles, wicker baskets of shells, or painted seaside bowls will emphasize the presence of the sea and will help to ground the room.

Sea sponges and natural loofahs are wonderful materials for bathrooms. Because they are natural products they will encourage movement of chi and can help to scrub away any negativity of the day while you are washing in the bath or shower.

Sensuous aromas soothe the senses and lift the spirits when you are soaking in the bath. Burn your favorite essential oil or put a few drops in the bath. Geranium and lavender are blissfully relaxing while ylang ylang and patchouli can add a taste of passion and romance. Scented soaps and fragrant bath balls cosset and embrace you and let you drift off into a drowsy, fragrant world of your own.

RIGHT Burning some candles in the bathroom creates a warm, sensuous glow when bathing. Candles also boost the sluggish energy flow that exists here.

SCENTED INCENSE CONES
Light some scented incense cones to fill the bathroom with a wonderful aroma so that you can relax and soak away all the worries of the day.

AROMATIC BATHROOM SOAPS
Place colorful and aromatic soaps in your bathroom to scent the atmosphere, to inspire your soul, and to liven up an otherwise neutral decor.

BOWL OF PEBBLES FOR GROUNDING
A bowl of assorted pebbles can bring in some grounding energy to the bathroom. They can also be made part of a seaside decorating scheme.

DECORATING ACCENTS
Natural starfish, sea sponges, and shells evoke a feeling of the sea in the bathroom. Line up some of them around the bath or display them prominently on shelves.

DELIGHT THE SENSES
Lift your senses in the bathroom by burning some aromatic essential oils. Use rose or jasmine to relax and calm, or lemon or lime if you need a pick-me-up.

NATURAL BATHROOM MATERIALS
A loofah or a body brush can be used to stimulate the body's lymph system and help it to eliminate toxins. They are also good for scrubbing away the worries of the day.

THE BEDROOM

YOUR BEDROOM IS one of the most important rooms in the home as it is here that your body rests and your spirit is revived, safe from the cares of the day. As you sink into a comfortable bed, you can feel cocooned from the world and allow yourself to be nurtured by this peaceful, calm space. It is also a special place of romance, where you share secrets and intimate moments with an adored partner.

A calm yin environment with minimal electrical equipment is what you are seeking in the bedroom. Restful pastel colors, flowing natural fabrics, carpeting or softwood flooring, and a comfortable, supportive, and well-positioned bed (see pages 134–135) are essential here to encourage a restorative, gentle flow of chi. Little furniture is needed to allow this energy to take its meandering course around the room.

Clutter has no place here, particularly on top of wardrobes or under the bed, where it can disturb your sleep. Surfaces and flooring that are full of discarded possessions or clothes will just breed stagnancy and hinder the movement of energy, denying you the rest and rejuvenation you need, so efficient storage is essential (see pages 132–133).

By burning some scented candles before you go to bed (being careful to extinguish them before you settle down to sleep) you can surround yourself with a restful aura, letting your body and soul drift off into a blissful, contented sleep.

A SENSUOUS SANCTUARY

Your bedroom is your personal retreat from the world. This is the place where you can spend afternoons reading, writing letters to friends, taking a nap, or having a long, revitalizing sleep. Here you should feel cosseted and loved, surrounded by tactile soft furnishings. The style of decoration in your bedroom is important so that you feel safe, secure, and peaceful the minute you walk in. Allow no work or computers here; this space is about winding down, relaxation, and tranquil dreams.

Bed bliss

Choose a good bed with a natural, comfortable, and supportive mattress. Wooden beds with a round, solid, or padded supportive headboard are best, as they only subtly affect chi movement.

The best position for the bed is diagonally opposite the door so that you can see people coming in. If you have no choice but to position the bed opposite the door, put a blanket box or a chest of drawers in front of it to slow down the incoming chi. Wake up happy each morning by

Having a chair in a large bedroom means you can snooze or read in this peaceful space in the daytime.

LEFT Have only one mirror in the bedroom, as mirrors are very yang. Position it on a side wall, never opposite the bed.

positioning an inspiring picture opposite the bed, but never hang pictures over the bed as you will subconsciously feel that they will fall on you. Placing your bed against a solid wall will make you feel secure, but if it is under a window you can feel unsettled. If you have no choice, fit both a shade and curtains at the window for symbolic support.

On reflection

Never position a mirror opposite the bed or have mirrored closet doors in that position as they are too energetic and can make you sleep fitfully.

If they are already fitted, then cover them at night with some muslin or another light material to lessen their effects. The Chinese believe that your soul goes astral traveling during sleep, and if it comes back to your body and sees its reflection in the mirror it can get a fright and not connect with you again. Mirrors in this position are also believed to encourage infidelity by introducing a third person into the relationship. If you must have a mirror in the room, hang it on a side wall.

A television has the same effect as mirrors and is too yang for the bedroom. Either remove it or cover it at night and turn it off. Leaving it on standby will still create an electromagnetic field, which you want to avoid in this peaceful and calm environment.

White walls bring in calming energy in an Earth bedroom.

A solid headboard gives you support while you are sleeping.

Placing lamps either side of the bed creates balance and harmony.

Silky pillows help to cosset you in the bedroom.

Positioning the bed diagonally opposite the door allows you to see people coming in.

Clutter checklist

Clutter overload in the bedroom can make you suffer from restless or broken sleep, so check to see if any clutter is lingering in the following places, and discard what is not needed. Look for the following:

✦ Clutter under the bed can disrupt your love life, so check under the bed for broken shoes, discarded food, clothes, or unused junk, and then either throw it out or give it away. Store only bedlinen here.

✦ Check your closets and give away to thrift shops anything that hasn't been worn for a year or no longer fits.

✦ Try to free up the top of any wardrobes—put boxes, bedding, or cases that are there somewhere else, as you will always feel they are going to fall on you.

✦ Go through your dressing table and de-junk any out-of-date cosmetics or scents. Throw away congealed lipsticks, ancient nail polishes, or gungy foundations to make room for current makeup that suits you.

WHAT NOT TO DO
If you place pictures over the bed, you will subconsciously always feel that they are going to fall on your head. Having too many books is overwhelming in what is meant to be a calm space.

LEFT Have bedroom cabinets on either side of the bed to store your bedside reading, candles, or crystals.

Turn down the vibes

It can be lovely to play some romantic or soulful music in the bedroom but every piece of electrical equipment gives out an electromagnetic field that can disturb your sleep. Either remove the player at night or unplug it at the wall. Because of the effect these EMFs can have on restorative sleep, keep as little electrical equipment as possible in the bedroom. Even small clock radios give out a strong field, so do not place one within 3m/10ft of your head—or use a simple battery alarm clock instead.

LEFT Having a pile of soft, tactile pillows on the bed will make it a cozier, more inviting environment.

LEFT Instead of a clock radio, use a battery alarm clock as it will give off less electromagnetic energy.

BELOW A woven cane headboard on a bed can give it a distinctive style.

Increase the passion

The vibrations of soft pastel colors are just right for the mood of the bedroom. Powder blues, greens, and violets calm the body, inducing a feeling of serenity. To inject some passion into the bedroom, paint the room orange or pink—a strong red can be too overwhelming unless you are very young.

Soft candlelight and lighting from bedside lamps will increase the yang energy to stimulate your libido. To further stimulate the loving vibrations, place a ruby crystal under your pillow and let its emanations open up your heart chakra.

BELOW You can bring some Fire energy into an Earth bedroom with a bedspread, as long as the bedlinen is white (the calming energy).

RIGHT This fluffy pink stool used as a bedside table adds some girlie glamour. Pink is ideal for calming a Wood bedroom.

STORAGE TO RESTORE CALM

Choosing the right storage for the bedroom can help to induce peace and tranquility in this yin space. To avoid disturbing your rest with any cutting chi from sharp corners, seek out furniture with rounded corners. Place bedroom cabinets either side of the bed for storing bedside reading and to create balance and harmony.

Choose softwood wardrobes and drawer units to enhance the calm atmosphere, or buy some wicker, rattan or seagrass units as they too are very yin. Sweaters, T-shirts, and blouses not only look good stored in open shelving units, but you can also see everything at a glance. Blanket boxes can accommodate spare bedlinen and pillows, and if sited at the bottom of the bed can deflect bad chi that emanates from the door or awkward corners. Storing anything under the bed is not recommended, but if you are short on space, drawer units under the bed are acceptable to hold blankets and bedlinen, provided it is clean and well preserved. If you are installing new closets, plan your needs carefully, allowing for plenty of drawers or pull-out baskets to store underwear, scarves, belts, shoes, hosiery, and jewelry.

If you select painted or laminate units or closets, match their color to the room's element (see pages 20–21). For example, in a west bedroom choose white or metal units. For a calmer energy here, use the calming element, which for Metal rooms is blue or black as Water calms Metal in the Exhaustive cycle.

BELOW Well-planned closets in the bedroom neatly hold all your clothes. Be sure to allow for enough storage for sweaters, T-shirts and underwear.

USEFUL SLIMLINE UNITS
Slimline units can fit into unused corners to give you more space in which to store bedlinen, towels, or other items that do not fit in elsewhere.

CLEVER USE OF SPACE
When you are short of drawer and shelf space in the bedroom, try mounting a rail under a shelf so that you can fit in some hanging units to store more clothes.

UNDERBED STORAGE
Although not normally recommended in feng shui, you can have drawers under your bed if storage is limited, provided you store only clean bedlinen.

SHELVING STORAGE
Open shelving is a good idea if you like to have your sweaters, purses, and hats on display. However, it's even more crucial to keep them tidy.

BLANKET BOX STORAGE
Blanket boxes work well in country-style bedrooms. Placed at the end of the bed, they are ideal for storing extra towels, bedlinen, quilts, and blankets.

BEDS FOR BLISSFUL DREAMING

You spend a large proportion of your life in bed so it is worthwhile taking some time finding the right one. Softwood beds support the yin atmosphere of the bedroom, and so pine, spruce, and cedar are ideal. Otherwise, look out for natural hardwoods such as beech, birch, maple, and oak. Beds made of iron or brass are not recommended as they speed up chi energy and can attract electricity from nearby radiators. If you have an adored iron bed, slow down chi flow by using bedlinen in the color of the room's calming element (see pages 20–21). For example, for an Earth room use white bedlinen as Metal calms Earth in the Exhaustive cycle.

A round or oval solid headboard lets chi move smoothly around it and gives good support when you are sitting up in bed. Padded and rectangular headboards are fine but avoid slatted styles, as you will never feel comfortable. If you already have this style of headboard, put big, squashy bolsters up against it for comfort when reading in bed.

When buying a bed be sure to try lying on it in the shop, and choose a mattress that feels comfortable and is supportive. Opt for a natural filling such as horsehair, camel hair, silk, or wool rather than man-made materials, which can give off static. Metal springs affect the local magnetic field and can disrupt chi movement.

Natural comforters, blankets, and bedlinen made from pure cotton or linen will help you relax and are better to use than synthetics, which have a static charge that can make you feel drained.

LEFT A solid, padded headboard gives you support and feels comfortable when you are sitting up reading or having breakfast in bed.

STRIKING BEDSPREAD
A chic bedspread adds color and a sense of luxury to a hardwood bed. This beige cover supports an Earth room while the white bedlinen calms it.

TACTILE PILLOWS
The contrasting textures of silky, velvet, furry, or soft patterned pillows look good on the bed, and give the bedroom an inviting atmosphere.

ROMANTIC CANOPY
A floaty canopy of sheer fabric can be very romantic over a bed. The soft, flowing curtains slow down the energy and make you feel more secure.

NATURAL FIBERS ARE BEST
Natural cotton or linen sheets and pure wool or cotton blankets are the best types to use on your bed because they will help you to wind down and sleep better.

HEADBOARD CURVES
A modern or classic-style curved headboard can slow down the flow of chi in the bedroom. Prop large pillows up against it for more comfort.

COMFORTABLE MATTRESS
A deep, well-constructed, solid mattress will help you sleep better during the night. Make sure that you buy one that has a natural filling for restful sleep.

PROTECTIVE WINDOW TREATMENTS

Your bedroom is your cozy retreat where you can snuggle up in bed on an early night or lazy afternoon reading your favorite magazine or a good book. Your window treatments need to enhance this coziness, keeping out the cold and any chilly drafts.

If you live near a busy road, sound insulation will also be important as you will want the curtains to muffle the noise and slow down the chi entering through the window. Therefore, choose curtains in heavy fabrics such as velvet, damask, or lined linen.

If light reduction and insulation against sound and cold are not so important and you want to lighten up a dark room, you can choose long, flowing curtains in a lighter fabric, and leave them unlined. Muslins, silks, and light cottons lie in delicate ripples and will let the light penetrate the room. Whichever fabric you choose, the soft hanging folds of curtains will conceal any harsh corners and lines in a very structured bedroom.

Wooden Venetian blinds will give you privacy at night but when opened will let you see out, while still providing

protection from a busy street or unsightly view. Wooden louvered shutters have a similar effect.

The even folds of fabric in roman shades will let chi meander slowly into the room.Simple shades show off the lines of attractive period window frames. They slow down incoming chi without allowing it to stagnate, and when they are pulled up during the day they let in the maximum amount of light. Blend the color of your chosen window treatment to the calm decorating scheme of your room (see pages 20–21).

LEFT Light-coloured blinds will keep the room dark at night while letting in some light during the day. They will also help to calm an Earth bedroom.

GENTLE FOLDS OF A ROMAN SHADE
Roman shades insure a gentle movement of chi in this calm room. They can be pulled up halfway during the day to give some protection from bright sunlight.

ORIENTAL BLINDS IN THE BEDROOM
Bamboo and wicker blinds give an oriental feel to the bedroom. They do, however, let in more light, so you may want to use a plain white shade underneath.

FULL FLOWING CURTAINS
Traditional windows can look stunning with full curtains hanging from a pole and draped over a holdback. Layering two curtains in different colors adds interest and style.

LIGHTER CURTAIN FABRICS
You can lighten up a dark or small room with a lighter curtain fabric. Cotton, linen, and muslin will all let in light while concealing ugly corners or imperfections.

CURTAIN AND SHADE COMBINATION
If you live near a main road you may find that it works better to combine a shade with full curtains to give you more protection and to reduce noise levels.

SHADE FOR FIRE BEDROOM
The diamond pattern of this shade enhances the Fire element and so will benefit a bedroom in the south. It will also bring calming energy into a Wood bedroom.

CHILD'S ROOM

A CHILD'S SPACE is often a multipurpose room. During the day children want to have fun playing with their friends, listening to music, or playing computer games. At night the room can turn into a study and then into a sleeping zone. All these different activities need to be taken into consideration when planning the layout of your child's room.

Good sleep is particularly important for children as they are still developing mentally, physically, and spiritually. Zoning a child's room with screens or furniture is important to separate the yin chi in the sleeping area from the yang chi in the study and play zone, otherwise sleep could become restless and disturbed.

Toys, DVDs, or computer games left scattered around the room at night will encourage stagnant energies that can make children feel lethargic and lacking in motivation. Encourage children to tidy up every evening before bedtime, putting everything away in storage baskets or boxes (see pages 142–143).

Help your child to feel safe and secure in their bedroom by making it their special place. Decorate it in restful colors, adding soft bedlinen in inspiring or character patterns, bright storage units, and a snug bed that is sited well away from beams, pillars, or sloping ceilings.

A RETREAT FOR PLAY AND SLEEP

Children's rooms are their own personal havens. Here is where they can give rein to their creative abilities, play games, read, get to grips with their homework, entertain their friends, and listen to music in peace. But it is also a place of rest where the body renews itself and future dreams are made.

Zone the space

Although primarily a place of rest and a yin environment, a child's room needs stimulation for hobbies and activities and so will benefit from some yang energy. Good planning is essential to separate or zone these two areas, otherwise your child may suffer from an overstimulated brain at night. This is a big issue in a teenager's room.

White walls will bring calming energy into an Earth bedroom.

Side storage units are good for holding your child's favourite cuddly toys or bedtime animals.

White duvet covers are soothing and will calm the energy in an Earth bedroom in the north-east and south-west.

Keep the space under the bed clutterfree so that your child sleeps blissfully.

Use hanging storage bags for pajamas or slippers.

You can create a play space in the bedroom but try to keep it away from the yin energies of the bed.

Shutters can be closed at night to create a cozy environment and then opened in the daytime for a bright, airy space.

The best location for the bed or beds is diagonally opposite the door as this enables the child to see people coming into the room, giving a feeling of safety and security. Never place a bed under a beam, opposite a pillar, or under a sloping ceiling because they will suffer from the cutting chi aimed at the bed or from compression (a feeling of restriction in a confined space). Bunk beds are great for saving space in a room for two children but again compression is an issue for the child on the bottom bunk. Twin beds with solid headboards and rounded corners are a better option. Place them against a solid wall as it gives much more support than a window.

Zone the sleeping space from the play/work area with a screen or a tall bookcase to separate the yin and yang energies. If there is a computer, TV, and/or music system in the room, turn them all off at night to reduce their electromagnetic fields. Children are vulnerable to this radiation as their bodies are still developing.

Colors and textures

Pastel colors are a good option for a child's room, as posters, bright storage units, and bedlinen will lift the chi here anyway. Bright colors, such as red or yellow, can overstimulate an active child. Busy patterned curtains may have a similar effect, so choose solid-colored curtains or a simple shade, which will slow chi flow.

RIGHT Cube-shaped storage systems in striking colors can add interest to a teenager's bedroom and hold shoes, jumpers, T-shirts, and other clothing.

Clutter checklist

Too much clutter in a child's room can cause confusion and affect their sleep, so search for any junk black holes such as the following:

+ Check for abandoned toys and games. Throw out broken ones and pass on or give to hospitals any that are not used. Store the rest in bright-colored stacking boxes or crates.
+ Go through your child's clothes to find those items that are too small, and give them to younger children or the thrift shop.
+ Search through computer games with your child and check if you can sell or exchange the abandoned ones.
+ Look through your child's books, keep the favorites, and pass on discarded titles to other children or libraries.

ABOVE A desk, computer, and perhaps another space for drawing are normal in a child's bedroom now. But screen off the space from the bed, as it is very yang.

WHAT NOT TO DO

All children love having pets, but do not place an aquarium in their bedroom, as the water and the movement of the fish are too overpowering for this space. Similarly, a lot of toys on shelves can overwhelm.

STORAGE FOR GOOD CHI FLOW

Children of any age have a lot of paraphernalia, whether it is toys, school supplies, sports equipment, or computer accessories. If you have two children sharing a room, the problem is doubled.

Children are also notoriously untidy, so right from the start you need to get to grips with storage to suit the age of your child and their bedroom. If possible, choose pieces they will not outgrow.

If toys, games and other equipment are scattered all over the room, it will disrupt chi flow and affect your child's well-being. From an early age, train your children to put their toys away at night so they have a peaceful area in which to sleep.

Today there are many inventive storage units for children's rooms. Animal baskets or hammocks made out of mesh material are great for storing fluffy and soft toys. Versatile stacking coloured boxes can hold a mixture of games and toys. Wooden units with pull-out colored crates serve the same purpose.

Put up adequate shelving on the wall above a desk to stop possessions from being discarded on the floor. The shelves can accommodate anything from crayons and drawing materials to books, computer games, and CDs.

If you are short of space, fix hooks to the back of the door with some soft hanging storage bags to keep your child's room the organized den it should be.

LEFT Young girls in particular love to have plenty of outfits to dress in, so choose a mixture of storage that allows adequate hanging space with plenty of drawers. Make sure that a child can reach at least one of the hanging rails so that they get into good habits of putting clothes away.

BLANKET BOX STORAGE
A wooden blanket box is so useful in a child's bedroom. Toys, books, and games can all be stored here when not in use, and it can even double as a nightstand.

MOVABLE STORAGE UNITS
Storage containers that have casters can be moved around a child's bedroom when you are picking up toys and then stored neatly at the side.

FABRIC STORAGE BASKETS
Fabric or rush storage baskets are flexible enough to hold soft and hard toys. Store them neatly out of sight at the end of the day under a shelf.

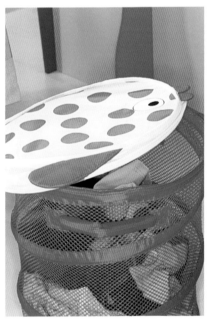

INDIVIDUAL DRAWER UNITS
Painting wooden storage units in animal or other themes makes them unique. This scheme suits a Metal bedroom, as Water (black) calms Metal.

FUN MESH BASKETS
Mesh baskets can be bought in animal and other fun shapes to hold clothes, soft toys, or shoes. They can sit on the floor or be hung on the back of a door.

SHELVING UNITS FOR BOOKS AND GAMES
Simple shelving units can store games, DVDs, computer games, and books for the older child. Try not to keep too many books in the bedroom as they are too yang.

DUVETS FOR PERFECT SLUMBER

Many children crave their favorite cartoon or action characters in bright colors on their duvet covers or comforters. This is fine provided fighting or other destruction is not depicted and the child generally sleeps well, as this type of bedcover can be very stimulating. If you have a child who has problems relaxing, it can be better to use the room's calming color on the bed (see pages 20–21). For example, if the room is a Water entrance (a north entrance) use a mid-green or a green-patterned comforter or duvet cover, as Wood calms Water in the Exhaustive cycle. Or, if your child has become difficult to control or is having temper tantrums, you could try using the controlling element; for example, in a Water room, have a yellow or beige duvet cover or comforter because Earth controls Water in the Destructive cycle.

You can also use the element colors and shapes (see pages 20–31) to influence the energy of the entire room. To support the existing energy in a Fire room, for example, you could use a pink duvet cover or comforter with a star or zigzag pattern, because these are among the colors and symbols for Fire. To calm the energy in an Earth room belonging to a boisterous child, you could have a white duvet cover or comforter with a circular silver or gold design as Metal calms Earth in the Exhaustive cycle. In a Metal room a wavy black or dark blue pattern on a light blue background will help your child slip into a peaceful sleep, because Water calms Metal in the Exhaustive cycle.

LEFT For a girl's bedroom with a south (Fire) entrance the bedcover could have a pink theme. Having triangular bunting over the bed also emphasizes the Fire energy.

DINOSAUR THEME DUVET COVER
For a child who loves films like Jurassic Park a duvet with a dinosaur theme can be the answer. Soft dinosaur toys surrounding the bed complete the scheme.

PLAIN PINK BEDCOVER
If your child has trouble sleeping in a Wood bedroom, buy a pink quilt, comforter, or duvet cover for some soothing energy, as Fire calms Wood in the element cycle.

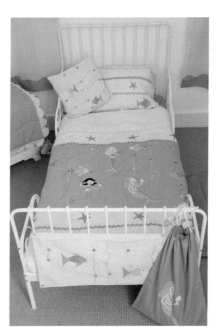

MERMAID THEME DUVET COVER
On a marine theme, lots of little girls are fascinated by mermaids. This duvet cover features mermaids and fish in the design and has a matching storage bag.

SEASIDE THEME BEDCOVER
If your child loves the seaside, choose a cover with a marine theme such as this quilt with its stylized waves, shells, starfish, octopus, and other sea creatures.

THE GARDEN

A GARDEN CAN BE a wonderful place in which to relax surrounded by luscious vegetation, glorious flowers, and shady trees. Gardens are not generally mapped out with the Pa Kua in feng shui—instead you work with the flowing shapes of nature to create harmony and balance around your home.

When you have a large garden, you can strengthen the protective guardian, the Black Tortoise at the back of the home, by growing some tall shrubs and trees. Meandering paths and curved borders are preferable to straight edges. If you have only a small paved courtyard garden, you can make it a success by keeping it well tended and featuring a mixture of healthy, colorful plants and tall, sweet-smelling climbers for privacy.

A fountain, pond, or other water feature in the front yard is very peaceful and cleansing and will encourage prosperity. Brighten up any dark yin areas in the front or back yard with bright strings of outdoor lights, solar lighting, or candles to stimulate the presence of more positive yang energy (see pages 154–155).

A RELAXATION ZONE

Your garden is your own natural haven where you can while away the hours planning changes, tending plants, relaxing in the sun, or entertaining friends for long summer lunches or evening barbecues. It is here that you escape all your worries by communing with nature and all living things.

Garden planning

When you are working out your garden design, insure that any trees or shrubs you are planning to grow will not block out any light, making your home dark or damp. Also check that they will not affect your property's foundations. Positioning some trees at the back of the garden will give support and protection, but resist planting a tree opposite the front door as it will act like a poison arrow at your entrance.

Allow for some curved beds around the lawn, and include a variety of plants of different heights here to create cohesion. Also vary the colors of the plants, mixing yang red, yellow, orange, and pink flowers with more yin blue, violet, and green plants for harmony and balance.

Allow paths to flow up to the front door and around the garden in a winding movement so that they emulate the movement of chi. Break up a straight path to your front door with pots or by letting plants grow over the edges, otherwise the energy will hit the entrance too fast and could detrimentally affect all living there. Straight paths elsewhere in the garden can be broken up in the same way.

Attractive lighting in the garden adds a fairy-tale quality and lifts the yang energies.

Surround the patio with a mixture of sweet-smelling flowers and aromatic evergreen plants.

LEFT Planning a pleasant eating area on the patio or lawn will allow for convivial lunchtime and evening meals during the summer months.

A round garden table is one of the most auspicious to use in feng shui.

Burning candles in the garden is very romantic and will boost energies while you are eating.

Keep out decay

Dead tree trunks, rotting vegetation, and weeds will lower the garden's vitality. If you can't immediately remove a dead tree trunk, put a chunk of natural quartz inside it to counteract the negativity there. Weeds or parasitic plants need to be tended every week or two, otherwise they could take over and strangle your garden, which in turn could make you feel stifled or restricted in your life.

Water features

A pond, fountain, or water feature in the front yard will enhance your prosperity and attract more chi through your front door. The best position is on the left-hand side as you look out of your home.

A swimming pool is very yin and can overwhelm a house if it is too large or is positioned too close to it. To stop this yin energy from seeping into the home, build a low wall around the pool or screen it with shrubs. A kidney-shaped pool that appears to hug the house is preferable to a rectangular pool.

Clutter checklist

A decaying, untidy, or overgrown garden makes you feel depressed and lacking in energy, so find any areas that are lowering your chi, such as the following:

✦ Check there are no overflowing garbage cans near your front door as they will deplete the vitality of the chi entering your home.

✦ Cut back overgrown shrubs and trees that are blocking your light at the front and preventing people from easily entering your home.

✦ Look for slugs, snails, or other pests that are eating your plants and vegetables, as they are symbolically sucking the goodness out of your life. Treat with organic remedies.

WHAT NOT TO DO
Although spiky plants are not so frowned on in the garden, their yang energies may be overpowering next to an eating area. Also, always grow several shrubs up trellis so that you don't feel threatened by neighbors.

Tall trees at the back of the garden give support and protection.

Growing perfumed shrubs up a wall will fill the patio with lovely aromas.

Having several pots of flowers or herbs adds color and interest on the patio.

A patio made from stone slabs will make you feel very grounded as they link to Earth energies.

High-backed garden chairs are not only comfortable, but will also help you feel secure.

FURNITURE FOR ENTERTAINING

Eating out in your garden is one of the pleasures of summer. Sitting and lazily enjoying a long lunch with good friends can be the perfect way of spending a summer's day. As entertaining is important to so many of us, choosing the most suitable garden furniture is essential.

Beneficial shapes and materials

A round table is best as it will not give off any cutting chi. Many garden tables are available in the octagonal shape of the Pa Kua, which is even more beneficial. Rectangular tables are also acceptable, but make sure that no one sits at the sharp corners. For vitality in the garden, buy yang hardwood furniture—or if you want a more relaxed atmosphere, opt for softwood, though it is less weatherproof. Metal furniture is more yang than hardwood and lasts better than wood if kept outside all year. Match chairs to the table and, where possible, choose curved styles, to encourage a good flow of chi.

Practical umbrellas

Make sure you buy an umbrella in a natural fabric, and choose one that is bigger than the table, to provide shade from the strong yang rays of a hot sun. Large colonial-style umbrellas are big enough to give shade to everyone sitting around the table.

BELOW An octagonal table is one of the most beneficial to have in the garden as it represents the shape of the Pa Kua, the main feng shui diagnostic tool.

ROUND TABLE IS AUSPICIOUS
A round table is one of the best to have in the garden as it symbolizes money. A canvas umbrella will provide welcome shade from the yang sun.

OVAL TABLE FOR GROUP EATING
An oval table with no sharp corners and with matching chairs encourages good chi flow. This table will feed big families and needs a correspondingly large umbrella.

GLASS TABLE FOR A MODERN SPACE
A rectangular glass table gives off yang energies in an outdoor "room." Matching it with metal chairs and containers adds a very modern style to the garden.

WICKER TABLE FOR A SMALL GARDEN
A small wicker table can be ideal when you have limited space in the garden. Chairs with curved arms will prevent any cutting chi being directed at guests.

GARDEN PLANTS FOR A VIBRANT SPACE

Sitting in a garden surrounded by glorious flowering plants, evergreens, and scented climbers is guaranteed to lift your spirits and soothe your soul.

Using the five elements

Work with the elements when planning your flower beds—either achieve harmony by using a balance of the five elements, or use a preponderance of the colors associated with each direction:

✦ Use red and pink plants in the south.

✦ Grow blue and violet ones in the north.

✦ Choose evergreens for the east and southeast.

✦ Go for white flowers in the west and northwest.

✦ Plant yellow and pale orange varieties in the southwest and northeast.

Celestial guardians

You can also support the ancient Chinese celestial guardians (see page 49) that surround your property. Plant small shrubs, such as camellias and roses, in the open Red Phoenix area in the south to bring luck into your life. A reliable camellia is *C. x williamsii* "Donation" (pink) or "Anticipation" (crimson). Traditional roses such as the pink "Louise Odier" are ideal.

In the east of the garden, ruled by the auspicious Green Dragon, the bearer of material success, grow taller shrubs such as hydrangeas, magnolias, or lilacs.

RIGHT Grow a mixture of yin and yang plants in the garden. Bright yellow and red flowers will bring in vibrant yang energies.

In the west, where the fiercely protective White Tiger resides, grow low plants, as the White Tiger must not overpower the Green Dragon. Combine bright or fragrant varieties, such as poppies and scented peonies, with low-growing shrubs.

For support in the north from the protective Black Tortoise, grow some climbers. Fragrant jasmine or honeysuckle will scent the evening air, while wisteria and clematis can disguise boundaries, unattractive sheds, or other eyesores.

BRIGHT POTS OF RED FLOWERS
You can brighten up the south area of the garden by adding some pots that are full of red flowers, as red supports the Fire element that exists here.

SPLASHES OF COLOR IN THE WEST
Brightly colored flowers, such as these single peonies, can be combined with low-growing shrubs in the west of the garden, where the guardian the White Tiger resides.

WISTERIA FOR GOOD COVER
Wisteria is a wonderfully attractive climber. It is ideal for covering up a wall or fence that is unattractive or which is quite old.

CLEMATIS IN THE NORTH
Tall shrubs and climbers can be grown in the north of the garden, which is ruled by the protective Black Tortoise.

SWEET-SMELLING FLOWERS
Jasmine is a fabulous plant to have in the garden as its glorious scent will fill the air when you are having alfresco suppers.

POTS, PATIOS, AND LIGHTING TO LIFT GARDEN CHI

Perhaps the most important part of your garden, whether it is big or small, is the patio, where you entertain friends or spend some leisurely time reading the newspapers on a sunny morning.

Natural materials

A patio made from stone slabs is hard-wearing and very grounding. It is particularly suitable for a garden in the southwest or northeast, both of which are associated with the Earth element. It is important that the stone slabs are not broken or in poor condition.

A popular alternative to stone, a wooden deck smooths the flow of chi. It looks good in most gardens but will particularly enhance those situated in the east and southeast. However, it can need more maintenance than stone to keep it looking good.

Ceramic and clay pots bring in solid Earth energy. They make a patio come alive, especially when filled with brightly colored flowering plants and wonderfully scented herbs. Include tall pots as well as some small ones in different shapes to create diversity.

Patio lighting

Lighting is the final element to make your patio space complete. Lights bring in some yang energy for alfresco meals at night and can also be used to highlight seasonal planting in flower beds. Garden flares, candles, votives in colored jars, and strings of small outdoor lights add a softer glow of light, which can encourage more relaxed dining. Think about buying some solar lights, which are readily available and will save energy.

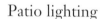

LEFT An attractive patio area that looks out on a rockery, pond, water feature, or other well-planned garden space will be used time and time again.

GROUNDING STONE SCULPTURE
A stone sculpture can look stunning in a garden, especially when it is cared for and well lit. It will also bring in some grounding Earth energy.

GARDEN CANDLES TO BOOST ENERGY
Candles in containers that can be pushed intothe earth like stakes can give soft lighting where it is needed. They will also lift the garden energy.

WELL-LIT PATH
A winding, well-lit path from your home to a patio eating area in another part of the garden will encourage a positive flow of chi to this sociable area.

WOOD AND WATER FOR GOOD CHI
A wooden deck is warm underfoot and encourages good chi flow. Adding an interesting water feature, even a small one, brings in more good chi.

POTS ON THE PATIO
Terra-cotta pots full of lovely flowering plants can adorn your patio space. The grounding energy of the pots will be balanced by the uplifting plant energy.

Index

PHOTOGRAPHY CREDITS

Key: ph= photographer, a=above, b=below, r=right, l=left, c=center, RPS=Ryland Peters and Small

p. 1 ph David Brittain/RPS; 2 ph Jan Baldwin/RPS/architecture by Totem Design, interior design by Henri Fitzwilliam-Lay and Totem Design (hfitz@hotmail.com & www.totem-uk.com); p. 3 ML Harris/Getty; 5 ph David Montgomery/RPS; p. 6 Keith Scott Morton/Red Cover; p. 7 a Gregor Schuster/Getty, br DEA/C.DANI/Getty, mr GK Hart/Vicky Hart/Getty, c Jake Fitzjones/Red Cover, bl fancy/photolibrary.com, bc Marks & Spencer; p. 8 Winfried Heinze/Red Cover; p. 9 a Winfried Heinze/Red Cover, br Guy Bouchet-Cardinale/Photononstop/ photolibrary.com; p. 10 c Grey Crawford/Red Cover, b Simon Brown/CICO Books, 10 a ML Harris/Getty; p. 11 Henry Wilson/Red Cover; p. 12 corbis/photolibrary.com; p. 13 b Greg Elms/Getty, 13al ph Caroline Arber/RPS; p. 14 Winfried Heinze/Red Cover; p. 15 b Verity Welstead/Red Cover, p. 15 a Stockbyte/Getty; p. 16 a Aleruaro/Getty, 16b ph Ray Main/RPS/David & Claudia Dorrell's apartment in London designed in conjunction with McDowell + Benedetti (www.mcdowell benedetti.com); p. 17 br Tim Evan-Cook/Red Cover, l ph Polly Wreford/RPS; p. 18 al Ryan McVay/Getty, al ph Debi Treloar/RPS/ Susan Cropper's family home in London, b ph Sandra Lane/RPS; p. 20 ac Michele Constantini/photolibrary.com, bl corbis/photolibrary.com, br Stockbyte/Getty, ml DAJ/Getty, mr Rosemary Calvert/Getty; p. 21 Trine Thorsen/Red Cover; p. 22 a Fabio Lombrici/Red Cover, b ph Debi Treloar/RPS; p. 23 a Ryan McVay/Getty, b Trine Thorsen/Getty, bl Diffused Diffused/photolibrary.com, c Marks & Spencer; p. 24 Paul Massey/Red Cover, a Keith Scott Morton/Getty; p. 25 bl Geoff Dann/ CICO Books, al Arne Pastoor/photolibrary.com, c Steve Cole/Getty, ar ph Henry Bourne/RPS, br ph Andrew Wood/RPS; p. 26 A Kompatscher/photolibrary.com; p. 27 ac Ryan McVay/Getty, b Guy Bouchet-Cardinale/Photononstop/photolibrary.com, c Marks & Spencer, ar ph Sandra Lane/RPS; p. 28 ar Johner/Getty, bl Lenora Gim/Getty; p. 29 a Datacraft/Getty, bc ph Debi Treloar/RPS, br ph David Loftus/RPS; p. 30 a C Squared Studios/Getty, b Jules Frazier; p. 31 al N Minh & J Wass/ Getty, bl ZenShui/Michele Constantini/Getty, bl Marks & Spencer, ar The Pier; p. 32 l Ken Hayden/Red Cover, r Jean Maurice/Red Cover; p. 33 IMAGEMORE Co., Ltd./Getty; 34 b ph Dan Duchars/RPS/architect Haifa Hammami's home in London; pp. 34-35 a ph Polly Wreford/RPS; p. 35 ar altrendo images/Getty, br Nonstock Images/photolibrary.com; p. 36 b Stockbyte/Getty; pp. 36-37 Ichou/photolibaray.com; p. 37 b Stewart Cohen/photolibaray.com; p. 38 Darrell Jones/Getty; p. 39 a Imagestate Ltd/photolibrary.com, c Riley Jon/photolibaray.com, b Creatas/ photolibrary.com; p. 40 b Digital Vision/photolibrary.com; pp. 40-41 Bruce Ayres/Getty; p. 41 r Stockbyte/photolibrary.com; p. 42 a altrendo images/Getty, b ph David Montgomery/RPS; p. 42-43 ph Polly Wreford/ RPS; p. 44 Brandon Harman/Getty; p. 45 a JGI/Getty, b William King/Getty, p. 45 c Nordic Photos/photolibrary.com; p. 46 Vicky Kasala/Getty; p. 47 a Tom Stoddart Archive/Getty, br Siwik Siwik/ photolibrary.com; p. 48 a redcover.com, b ph Henry Bourne/RPS; p. 49 tl Geoff Dann/CICO Books, 49 cl Corbis/photolibrary.com; p. 50 a Flora Press/photolibrary.com b Andrew Lord/ photolibrary.com; p. 51 r Ron Evans/Red Cover, p. 51 bl C Squared Studios/Getty; p. 52 The Pier; p. 53 Fancy/photolibrary.com; p. 54 all Geoff Dann/CICO Books; p. 55 r Jean Maurice/Red Cover, a Lottie Davies/Getty; p. 60 Simon Brown/ CICO Books; p. 61 a Ulrika Malm/Getty, b Jutta Klee/Getty; p. 62 b Simon Brown/Getty, a ph Chris Everard/RPS; p. 63 all images Gary Powell/Getty; p. 64 Huntley Hedworth/Getty; p. 65 a Janis Christie/Getty, b David Cooper/Getty; p. 66 Trinette Reed/Getty; p. 67 a & b Geoff Dann/CICO Books; p. 68 b ph David Montgomery/RPS; p. 69 al Geoff Dann/CICO Books; p. 70 a ML Harris/Getty, c Alexandra Rowley/Getty, b Warren Smith/Getty; p. 71 Henry Wilson/Red Cover; p. 72 l Sian Irvine/ Getty, r ph Jan Baldwin/RPS/a family home in London-architecture by Nicholas Helm and Yasuyuki Fukuda (architectural assistant) of Helm Architects (www.helmarchitects.com), interior design & all material finishes supplied by Maria Speake of Retrouvius Reclamation & Design (www.retrouvius.com); p. 73 b Karyn Millet/Red Cover, a Keith Scott Morton/Getty; p. 74 cr Cheung Jennifer/photolibrary.com, l ph Jan Baldwin/RPS/Mark Smith's home in the Cotswolds (info@smithcreative.net), ar ph Tom Leighton/RPS; p. 75 al ph Polly Wreford/RPS, ar ph Chris Everard/RPS/www.emmabridgewater.co.uk, b ph Jan Baldwin/RPS/ designed by Mullman Seidman Architects (www.mullmanseidman.com); p. 76 a ph Tom Leighton/RPS/a loft in London designed by Robert Dye Associates (www.robertdye.com), b Jo-Ann Richards/Getty; p. 77 l ph Pia Tryde/RPS; r ph Jonathan Buckley/RPS; p. 78 l Simon McBride/Red Cover, c Andersen Ross/Getty; pp. 78-79 main ph Debi Treloar/RPS/Paul Balland and Jane Wadham of jwflowers.com's family home in London; pp. 80-81 main ph Christopher Drake/RPS/Valentina Albini's home in Milan; p. 81 a Jake Fitzjones/Red Cover, b Huntley Hedworth/Getty; p. 82 ph Christopher Drake/RPS/Gosia Rojek Interiors (+1 718 802 0722) townhouse in Brooklyn Heights, architectural work by DiDonno Associates Architects, P.C (didonno.associates@attglobal.net); p. 83 al ph Andrew Wood/RPS; ac ph Debi Treloar/RPS; ar ph Andrew Wood/RPS; bl ph Christopher Drake/RPS /Fiona & Woody Woodhouse's 16th century weatherboard cottage in Surrey, designed by Bexon Woodhouse Creative (www.bexonwoodhouse.com), br Michael Dunne/www.ewastock.com; p. 84 c Siri Stafford/Getty, l ph Andrew Wood/RPS/Nanna Ditzel's home in

Copenhagen (www.nanna-ditzel-design.dk); pp. 84-85 ph Debi Treloar/ Nicky Phillips' apartment in London; pp. 86-87 main ph Chris Everard/ RPS /interior designer Ann Boyd's own apartment in London (020 7351 4098); p. 87 a Per Magnus Persson/Getty, b Ryan McVay/Getty; p. 88 l ph Chris Everard/RPS /Jonathan Wilson's apartment in London, light courtesy of SCP, r Dwell; p. 89 a The Pier, b Noel Hendrickson/Getty, cr GoGo Images/photolibrary.com; p. 90 Tom Merton/Getty; p. 91 al James Tse Photography Inc/photolibrary.com, bl McCoy Aaron/photolibrary.com, ac ph Christopher Drake/designed by McLean Quinlan Architects (www.mcleanquinlan.com), ar The Pier, br Dwell; p. 92 ph Jan Baldwin/ RPS/Emma Wilson's house in London (www.45crossleyst.com); p. 93 al ph Catherine Gratwicke/RPS/Elena Colombo's apartment in New York, ac ph Debi Treloar/RPS/Nicky Phillips' apartment in London, bl ph Debi Treloar/RPS/designer Susanne Rutzou's home in Copenhagen (www.rutzou.com), bc ph Jan Baldwin/RPS/interior designer Didier Gomez's apartment in Paris (orygomez@free.fr), br ph Polly Wreford/ RPS/Kathy Moskal's apartment in New York designed by Ken Foreman (www.kenforemandesign.com), ar Dwell; p. 94 Aura/Getty; p. 95 br The Pier, al Cotswold Company, bl, bc & ar The Holding Company, ac ph Polly Wreford/RPS/Adria Ellis' apartment in New York; p. 96 ph Polly Wreford/RPS/Daniel Jasiak's apartment in Paris; p. 97 bl & bc ph Debi Treloar/RPS, al Johnny Bouchier/Getty, ac Pia Tryde/Getty, ar Jean Maurice/Getty, br Catherine Servel/Getty; p. 98 b 136566/Getty, c Jun Yamashita/ailead/Getty; p. 99 Ikea; p. 100 Lombok; p. 101 a Ivan Hunter/Getty, bl Jo-Ann Richards/Getty, br Amanda Turner; p. 102 Ken Hayden/Getty; p. 103 ar RK Studio/Getty, ML Harris/Getty, bc Christine Bauer/Red Cover, al ph David Loftus/RPS, ac & br Marks & Spencer; p. 104 ph David Montgomery/RPS/a house in Connecticut designed by Lynn Morgan Design (www.lynnmorgandesign.com); p. 105 al IPS Co Limited/photolibrary.com, br Chris Ryan/Getty, ac ph Chris Everard/RPS/ Jamie Drake's Manhattan apartment (www.drakedesignassociates.com), ar ph David Loftus, bl The Cotswold Company; p. 106 l ph Jan Baldwin, r ph Jan Baldwin/RPS/architecture by Totem Design, interior design by Henri Fitzwilliam-Lay and Totem Design (hfitz@hotmail.com & www.totem-uk.com); pp. 106-107 ph Debi Treloar/Nicky Phillips' apartment in London; p. 108 Rosanne Olson/Getty; p. 109 a Kim Sayer/Red Cover, b Stewart O'Shields/Getty; p. 110 ph Christopher Drake/RPS/architecture by Voon Wong Architects, interior design by Florence Lim (www.voon-benson.com); p. 111 al Jake Fitzjones/Getty, am Peter Anderson/Getty, ar Simon McBride/Getty, bc Jake Fitzjones/Getty, bl Ikea, br The Cotswold Company; p. 112 ph Christopher Drake/a house in Salisbury designed by Helen Ellery of The Plot London (www.theplotlondon.com); p. 113 al ph Dan Duchars/RPS, ac ph Chris Everard/RPS, br ph Christopher Drake/ RPS, bl redcover.com/Getty, ar The Holding Company; p. 114 ph James

Merrell/Christine Walsh and Ian Bartlett's house in London designed by Jack Ingham of Bookworks; p. 115 al Janis Christie/Getty, am Andersen Ross/Getty, al Inti St. Clair/Getty, bl Ivan Hunter/Getty, bc ph Chris Everard, br Fired Earth; p. 116 l Henry Wilson/Red Cover, br Victoria Snowber/Getty; pp. 116-117 Fired Earth; p. 118 bl Meredith Heuer; pp. 118-119 Fired Earth; p. 119 br Digital Vision; p. 120 Fired Earth; p. 121 al Digital Vision/Getty, am Jake Fitzjones/Getty, bl Ivan Hunter/Getty, br Bieke Claessens/Getty, ar Fired Earth, bc ph Andrew Wood/RPS; p. 122 Fired Earth; p. 123 al & ar Fired Earth, ar Lisa M. Robinson/Getty, bl Alex Wilson/Getty, br Nancy R. Cohen/Getty, bc ph James Merrell; p. 124 Datacraft/Getty; p. 125 al IMAGEMORE Co., Ltd./Getty, ar Gregor Schuster/Getty, bl David Loftus/Getty, bm IMAGEMORE Co., Ltd./Getty, ac ph David Montgomery/RPS, br ph David Montgomery/RPS; p. 126 l ph Sandra Lane/RPS/Harriet Scott of R.K. Alliston's apartment in London (www.rkalliston.com), c ph Sandra Lane/RPS/Sophie Eadie's family home in London; pp. 126-127 main ph Chris Everard/RPS/interior designer Ann Boyd's own apartment in London(020 7351 4098); p. 128 bl James Mitchell/Getty, a Simon McBride/Red Cover; p. 129 bl Thomas Northcut/ Getty, br Robert Warren/Getty; p. 130 al ph Sandra Lane/RPS/Sophie Eadie's family home in London, b Hatty Lane-Fox's house in London, cr Ed Reeve/Getty; p. 131 ar Jean Maurice, b The Pier; p. 132 Ikea; p. 133 bl designed by Helen Ellery of The Plot London (www.theplotlondon.com), br ph Henry Bourne/RPS, ar Lucinda Symons/CICO Books, al Andersen Ross/Getty, am Lucinda Symons/Getty; p. 134 ph Jan Baldwin/RPS/ Wendy Jansen and Chris Van Eldik, owners of J.O.B. Interieur's house in Wijk bij Duurstede, The Netherlands (JOBINT@xs4all.nl); p. 135 bl ph David Montgomery/RPS/a House in South London designed by Todhunter Earle Interiors (www.todhunterearle.com), bc ph Debi Treloar/ RPS/owner's of Maisonette, Martin Barrell & Amanda Sellers' home in London, al The Pier, ac Ilva, ar Lombok, br Lena Koller/Getty; p. 136 ph Polly Eltes/RPS/a house in London designed by Charlotte Crosland Interiors (www.charlottecrosland.com); p. 137 bl ph David Montgomery/ RPS/Blakes Lodging designed by Jeanie Blake (www.blakesbb.com), bc ph Polly Eltes/RPS/Emily Todhunter's house in London designed by Todhunter Earle Interiors (www.todhunterearle.com), al Henry Wilson/ Red Cover, ar Steve Hawkins/www.ewastock.com, br Di Lewis/ www.ewastock.com, ac MAISANT Ludovic/photolibrary.com; p. 138 bl redcover.com/Getty, br redcover.com/Getty; p. 139 The Cotswold Company; pp. 140-141 The White Company; p. 141 bl ph Dan Duchars/RPS/architects Patrick Theis & Soraya Khan's home in London (www.theisandkhan.com), ar Vincent Leblic/photolibrary.com, br 136566 /Getty; p. 142 Thomas Northcut/Getty; p. 143 al redcover.com/Getty, am redcover.com/Getty, bl redcover.com/Getty, ar ph Debi Treloar/RPS, bc Ikea, br The White Company; p. 144 The White Company;

p. 145 ar, br & bl Babyface, ar ph Sandra Lane; p. 146 c ph Jonathan Buckley/RPS, Peter Samuels/Getty; p. 147 Tino Tedaldi/CICO Books; p. 148 bl Ken Hayden/Getty, c Ivan Hunter/Getty; p. 149 br Tino Tedaldi/CICO Books; p. 150 Andy Sotiriou/Getty; p. 151 br ph Tom Leighton/RPS, al Tino Tedaldi/CICO Books, bl Juliet Greene/photolibrary.com, ar Mats Hallgren/Getty; p. 152 Darrell Gulin/Getty; p. 153 ar Jacqui Hurst/Getty, bl James Randklev/Getty, br Vincenzo Lombardo/Getty, al Tino Tedaldi/CICO Books, bc ph Pia Tryde/RPS; p. 154 Rob Melnychuk/Getty; p. 155 al ph Melanie Eclare/RPS/lighting designed by Sally Storey (www.johncullenlighting.co.uk), ac ph Christopher Drake/RPS, ar Reto Guntli/Red Cover, bl John Glover/photolibrary.com, br Tino Tedaldi/CICO Books.

Every effort has been made to trace the copyright holder of each image. Please contact the publisher with any queries regarding credits.

ILLUSTRATION CREDITS

p. 8 al Stephen Dew; p. 13 all artwork Stephen Dew; p. 14 br Trina Dalziel; p. 14 ar Trina Dalziel; p. 22 ar Cathy Brear; p. 24 ar Cathy Brear; p. 26 ar Cathy Brear; p. 28 ar Cathy Brear; p. 30 ar Cathy Brear; p. 33 al Stephen Dew; p. 34 al Stephen Dew; p. 36 al Stephen Dew; p. 38 al Stephen Dew; p. 40 al Stephen Dew; p. 42 al Stephen Dew; p. 44 al Stephen Dew; p. 46 al Stephen Dew; p. 49 ar Cathy Brear, b Trina Dalziel; p. 51 al Stephen Dew; p. 56 Stephen Dew; p. 57 Stephen Dew; p. 58 all Stephen Dew; p. 59 all Stephen Dew; p. 61 t Trina Dalziel; p. 63 all Trina Dalziel; p. 64 Trina Dalziel; p. 65 b Trina Dalziel; p. 68 t Trina Dalziel; p. 69 ar, bl, br Trina Dalziel; p. 74 bc Stephen Dew

Publisher's Acknowledgments

Babyface
www.babyface.uk.com
+44 (0)1483 720734

Fired Earth
www.firedearth.com
+44 (0)1295 810832

ILVA
www.ilva.co.uk
+44 (0)845 245 8285

The Pier
www.pier.co.uk
+44 (0)845 609 2134

The Cotswold Company
www.cotswoldco.com
+44 (0)161 688 1671

Holding Company
www.theholdingcompany.co.uk
+44 (0)20 8445 2888

Lombok
www.lombok.co.uk
+44 (0)870 240 7380

The White Company
www.thewhitecompany.com
+44 (0)870 900 9555

Dwell
www.dwell.co.uk
+44 (0)870 241 8653

IKEA
www.ikea.com
1-800-434 IKEA

Marks and Spencer
www.marksandspencer.com
+44 (0)1925 672317

Author Acknowledgments

I would like to thank Liz Dean for her friendship and creative support in this project. A special thank you to my family in Portugal—Simon, Emma, Marina, and my sister Gill for their encouragement in the lonely writing process. Finally to all my friends, particularly Claire M, Claire G, Anna, Paul, and all my new Brighton pals who made sure I went out and had some fun during the writing process.

Mary Lambert is currently based in Brighton, England, and can be contacted for feng shui and decluttering consultations for homes and businesses via her website: www.marylambertfengshui.com.